TRANSFORMING MIND

Recent Titles in the Series in Language and Ideology

Transforming Mind

A Critical Cognitive Activity

GLORIA GANNAWAY

Series in Language and Ideology
Edited by Donaldo Macedo

BERGIN & GARVEY
Westport, Connecticut • London

Library of Congress Cataloging-in-Publication Data

Gannaway, Gloria.
    Transforming mind : a critical cognitive activity / Gloria
Gannaway.
        p.   cm. — (Series in language and ideology, ISSN 1069–6806)
    Includes bibliographical references and index.
    ISBN 0–89789–279–8 (alk. paper) — ISBN 0–89789–280–1 (alk. paper: pbk.)
    1. Critical pedagogy—United States.   2. Intercultural education—
United States.   3. Educational anthropology—United States.
    4. Literacy—United States.   I. Title.   II. Series.
    LC196.5.U6G36   1994
    370.19'2'0973—dc20   93–11854

British Library Cataloguing in Publication Data is available.

Library of Congress Catalog Card Number: 93–11854
ISBN: 0–89789–279–8
        0–89789–280–1 (pbk.)
ISSN: 1069–6806

First published in 1994

Bergin & Garvey, 88 Post Road West, Westport, CT 06881
An imprint of Greenwood Publishing Group, Inc.

Printed in the United States of America

The paper used in this book complies with the
Permanent Paper Standard issued by the National
Information Standards Organization (Z39.48–1984).

10 9 8 7 6 5 4 3 2 1

For my children,
Jenifer and Jeffrey

Contents

Foreword

Gloria Gannaway's *Transforming Mind: A Critical Cognitive Activity* brings to focus the debate over cultural literacy, a debate that recycles old assumptions and values regarding the meaning and usefulness of literacy. As Gannaway points out, cultural legionnaires such as E. D. Hirsch support the notion that cultural literacy is a matter of banking the values of our "common culture." This position, unfortunately, still informs the vast majority of educational programs and manifests its logic in the renewed emphasis on the romanticized "good old days" of our Western heritage.

For the notion of cultural literacy to become useful, it must be situated within a theory of cultural production and viewed as an integral part of the way in which people produce, transform, and reproduce meaning. Cultural literacy must be seen as a medium that constitutes and affirms the historical and existential moments of lived experience that produce a subordinate or lived culture. Hence, it is an eminently political phenomenon, and must be analyzed within the context of a theory of power relations and an understanding of social and cultural reproduction and production.

Gannaway's book challenges and deconstructs the process by

which Hirsch and others attempt to reconstitute history so as to put our "common Western culture" in an unrealistic light. A critical reading of our common Western culture would force us to juxtapose historical events in order to provide a cultural collage that makes us look at Western culture through a convex mirror. Simply put, Gannaway calls for a critical reading that will create a pedagogical space for readers to ask the victims—the Africans who endured the chains of slavery, the Indians who were victims of a quasi-genocide, the women who were historically treated as half-human, the Jews who were persecuted through the centuries, the Japanese who experienced firsthand the destructive power of Western civilization's scientific development—to reassess our so-called advanced civilization. If readers become critical so as to apply the same rigorous "objective" standards of science, intellectual honesty, and academic truth in their inquiry, they will arrive at a much more complex response than is allowed for in the prevailing version of our common cultural literacy. Gannaway argues against those educators who have invested in a dominant ideological system designed to produce power asymmetries along the lines of race, gender, class, culture, and ethnicity. She advocates a pedagogy that produces teachers who refuse such investments so as to be free to think more critically, thus recognizing the falsehoods embedded in the various literacy pedagogies created by the dominant class.

A critical cultural literacy pedagogy that includes Gannaway's critical cognitive activity paradigm will enable readers to understand how language plays an important role in transfiguring and distorting realities, which contributes to the reproduction of the dominant ideology that often informs education. The deconstruction of language challenges readers to recognize the insidiousness of the dominant ideology and its role in the domestication of the mind.

—Donaldo Macedo

Acknowledgments

Thanks to James Kinneavy and Douglas Kellner for their support over the years as professors and friends, and special thanks to Kellner for showing my work to Henry Giroux.

Thanks to Henry Giroux, Donaldo Macedo, Lynn Flint, and Jude Grant for their patience and enthusiastic help in improving and preparing the manuscript.

Thanks to my favorite postmodern artists, Laurie Anderson and Barbara Kruger, for giving me permission to dress up my book with their art.

Thanks to my good friends who were great sounding boards with lots of valuable suggestions, especially Kym Dorman, Joyce Daniels, and Rob Camp.

And, most of all, I thank my daughter, Jenifer, who has worked hard to keep me working and has been my unflagging reader and critic. Whatever is coherent in this book is largely due to her complete understanding of what I was trying to do, her ear for language, her wide-ranging intellectual power, and her witty loving support.

TRANSFORMING MIND

I

Defining the Problem

"Hello, excuse me, can you tell me where I am?"
—*Laurie Anderson**

American education is in the midst of a great crisis. It has been for years. Students are not learning the skills and knowledge they need to function effectively in today's complex and rapidly changing world. Serious inadequacies in the areas of reading, writing, math, and science are well documented, and there are indications of a dramatic lack of interest in the arts, philosophy, literature, and the social sciences as well. In addition, there is a huge drop-out problem and attendant social problems. I have been a college English teacher for over twenty years and I have observed an unmistakable deterioration in the cognitive development, academic standing, and social maturity of students coming out of the public school system.

Some say it depends on what schools you are talking about, and others say today's students know a lot but not, perhaps, what traditional tests give them a chance to show. I won't argue with either point, but some qualified generalizations can be

*From "Say Hello" by Laurie Anderson. © 1984 Difficult Music.

Photograph by Barbara Kruger, 1987. Used by permission.

made that can only be interpreted as extremely critical problems for American society. It is these problems that I am attempting in this book to define, analyze, and address.

The most influential response to the problems so far is the reactionary back-to-basics movement, with its emphasis on the traditional teaching of the "three Rs." In addition, there is the more "progressive" effort to accentuate the teaching of science and technology in order to make our society more competitive in the world market. These efforts are insufficient, for they fail to address the radical changes that have taken place in the world and in American culture.

In order to remedy the inadequacies in education, it is first essential to understand today's society and its problems. It is the purpose of this book to reveal and analyze the changes in our society that affect education. In search of a solution to the problems of education, I will argue the need not just for literacy in the narrow sense of minimal reading and writing skills, nor for computer literacy, but for cultural literacy in the largest sense. This includes political literacy and visual literacy and mass media literacy. As I will discuss later, the term "literacy" is not sufficient. I want a term that means creative critical thinking and action in connection with deconstructive reading of the texts of culture. The term I have come up with is "critical cognitive activity."

The term "critical cognitive activity" is derived from L. S. Vygotsky's theory of thought and language, which I will discuss at length in the last chapter. Vygotsky places at the center of education cognitive development—the development of higher mental processes. Cognitive development entails "activity"—an important concept in Vygotsky. "Activity" means the behavior patterns that society prescribes for a given situation. For Vygotsky, cognitive development, language—Vygotsky calls it "speech activity"—and socialization are inextricably intertwined. Learning takes place within educational "activities" designed to build the individual's abilities to comprehend socially significant tasks and to use effective strategies for undertaking them.

I want to say that American education needs a new paradigm on which our education system will be restructured according to the goal of teaching students to learn to be active participating members of society capable of understanding, critically analyzing, and creatively solving the problems of society. The critical cognitive activity paradigm will lay a new foundation for our education system, which will become able to produce *participating minds* instead of passive, ineffectual, underdeveloped minds unable to do anything more than make a feeble effort to sustain the social status quo.

First, I will discuss some of the current arguments in the debate on education reform. I will discuss E. D. Hirsch at length because his views are very popular in some quarters and are in many ways representative of mainstream thinking. Then I will discuss the views of two radical educators, Henry Giroux and Stanley Aronowitz, who make an overall analysis and critique of the current state of American education and outline their agenda for change.

E. D. HIRSCH'S CULTURAL LITERACY

E. D. Hirsch calls the deficit in cultural literacy "the great hidden problem" in American education (Hirsch 1987, 1). He claims that a decline in cultural literacy is the problem behind the literacy problem that currently plagues the American school system, a problem that he believes he has identified as the failure of schools to teach students, especially young students, the basic "facts" of American culture. He argues that he has rediscovered the "old truth" of the importance of knowing specific information; therefore, teachers must equip students with a set of information that he claims is shared by all literate persons in our society, giving them what he calls "cultural literacy," the basic information they need in today's world (xiii). For Hirsch, this cultural literacy will provide the essential basis for learning to read well and becoming well enough educated to communicate and function successfully in democratic society. "Only by piling up specific, communally shared information can children learn to participate in complex cooperative activities with other members of their community" (xv).

The basis for his argument is the following set of propositions: "a human group must have effective communications to function effectively"; "effective communications require shared culture"; "shared culture requires transmission of specific information to children" (xvii). Hirsch is convinced that schools are the primary transmitters of the needed cultural information, that they are not performing this function, and that adoption of his cultural literacy program is the means by which schools can begin to perform it. He is adamant that schools alone take the responsibility and the blame—not television, parents, or poverty.

Since "universal literacy is inseparable from democracy" (12), "it should energize people to learn that only a few hundred pages of information stand between the literate and the illiterate, between dependence and autonomy." The only "cost" of accepting his proposal, says Hirsch, is "simply the demystification of literate culture" (143), that is, admitting that everyone, not just the advantaged members of society, can learn what they need to know. Hence the title of his book: *Cultural Literacy: What Every American Needs to Know.*

Hirsch explains in the first paragraph of his preface that he is interested in cultural literacy primarily on behalf of the poor and illiterate, whose state he blames solely on the present-day "faulty education theories" that are forced upon our teachers. He charges that schools, practicing "romantic formalism," are teaching skills, not traditional American information. Hirsch maintains that reading is being taught as a skill and that content of schoolbooks is ignored.

He does not like what he says students are presently reading in their school curricula: "stories," "chapters from novels," "essays about human feelings," and "other selections of the kind." They are a waste of time. Students need "factual narratives" of traditional American lore. He claims that grade school students, including disadvantaged children, would benefit more from materials with "cultural content" than from those that "develop abstract skills" (27). Students need to know the same things in order to communicate with each other and, therefore, should not be given the "shopping mall" type of education they now have, which allows them to take diverse courses of little substance that add up to a "fragmented" education. Cultural content is important mostly because it is shared rather than because of any intrinsic value, and according to Hirsch, today's high school graduates do not know enough of the same information to communicate well with each other (8).

Hirsch asserts that no one lacks cognitive development, only information. He attacks the teaching of critical thinking on the two grounds that (1) students do not need it, and (2) critical thinking cannot be taught. He also implies that there is not room in the curriculum for both cultural literacy and critical thinking; moreover, his attitude toward proponents of critical thinking is highly confrontational, as if they are enemies of cultural literacy and good education. In one place he accuses the critical thinking movement of attacking the goal of teaching shared information (132), and in another place he claims that this attitude undermines its own progressive political and economic agenda (23–24).

Critical thinking is the main target, but Hirsch is opposed to the teaching of skills in general (62). For Hirsch, the focus on teaching "skills"—critical thinking, abstract thinking, and mental development—is a misguided "liberal," "progressive" agenda. He claims that studies prove that culturally disadvantaged students from fifth grade and from the community college level had all the necessary mental development to read well and lacked only background information, cultural literacy. (He obviously hasn't been in many community college freshman English classes!)

Hirsch is very scornful of "liberal" fears that teaching only "traditional information" is tantamount to indoctrination in a conservative point of view. He vigorously insists that shared items of traditional information are largely arbitrary "accidents of culture" created and reproduced in society in innocence and neutrality, and denies that they carry any political value charge whatsoever, but in another place, he makes this ambiguous and · seemingly contradictory statement: "Although teaching children national mainstream culture doesn't mean forcing them to accept its values uncritically, it does enable them to understand those values in order to predict the typical attitudes of other Americans" (24). He also admits that items on his list are accepted or rejected by the unidentified "culture makers" according to some scale or standard of judgment (84). (Shouldn't one be concerned about who is "making" culture, why, and in whose interest?)

Toward the end of the book, Hirsch seems to completely reverse his position with the problematical declaration that our schools "have a duty to teach widely accepted cultural values," but they also have a duty "*not* to take political stands on matters that are subjects of continuing debate" (137). It appears that he thinks his readers are too intellectually unsophisticated to see his blatant vagueness and inconsistency. (Perhaps he listened to too many Reagan speeches.)

I want to argue that there are many problems with Hirsch's position, one of which is that he denies that there are values inherent in traditional cultural literacy that imply a political stance toward the topical issues that affect everyone's present and future. Although I agree with Hirsch's basic point that reading and writing entail shared knowledge in addition to mechanical skills, my position is that Hirsch's program will promote traditional American ideology unless it is expanded to include alternative views, disclosure of biases, and strategies for critique. Moreover, regardless of Hirsch's intentions, it is easy to imagine his program being used to justify teaching only an ideologically biased list of "information" from an ideologically biased point of view, excluding any culturally marginal or critical material.

Hirsch recognizes that there is a problem with cultural literacy in American society, but I believe he has analyzed it incorrectly and, therefore, offers an ineffectual solution. I will continue my discussion of what I perceive to be the biggest problems with his argument, and then I will submit in the following chapters my own analysis and solution to the problem of cultural literacy.

The main problem with his analysis is that he doesn't recognize the radical changes in society brought about by the electronic age. It is very likely that in the electronic age, the age of information, people share much more information than ever before—it just isn't the information that appears on the cultural literacy tests Hirsch refers to. Instead, it is knowledge of popular culture, primarily disseminated through mass media.

Hirsch asserts that the key to communication is "shared" knowledge ("knowledge" and "information" appears to be synonymous), but it seems that, if that is the case, any shared knowledge will do—it doesn't have to be "traditional lore," as he claims. It can be knowledge of TV programs, popular music, movies, cars, fashion, the stock market, and football. If so, there is nothing to worry about. My response to his charge that high school students today don't share much information is that it is probable that they do, in fact, share a vast amount of information—information about popular culture that is not on the "list."

Hirsch is concerned that businessmen no longer allude to Shakespeare in their correspondence and, therefore, do not communicate as effectively, but aside from the fact that Hirsch's anecdotal evidence leaves room to doubt that American businessmen ever quoted Shakespeare as common practice, it is well established that the primary practical problem that plagues business communication as well as all professional communication is poor writing skills, not lack of shared knowledge. Though of course businessmen and everyone else would benefit from knowing Shakespeare, for establishing rapport, "How about those Dallas Cowboys?" should work just fine.

If Hirsch acknowledged that shared topical knowledge is also cultural literacy, he would, perhaps, be led to critique contemporary TV culture and to realize that social problems and cultural literacy are more complex and problematical than he thinks. He might also realize that his cultural literacy could most effectively be taught on TV in thousands of repeated "cultural literacy minutes" or on game shows. To dismiss the effects of TV in one sentence is to completely ignore the role of electronic technology in the actual dynamics of our society. Hirsch does not acknowledge that culture profoundly affects the way people think and learn as well as what they think, feel, and desire; nor does he acknowledge that American culture has changed or that education should track these changes and design methods for preparing students to understand, adapt to, and affect society.

Another problem is that Hirsch has an extremely shallow definition of cultural literacy. He states his goal as "mature literacy for *all* our citizens" (xiv), but literacy doesn't seem to go beyond universal "possession" of a "list of information actually possessed by literate Americans" (xv). Moreover, within the rather circular structure of his own argument, it would seem to be more logical to say that, if cultural literacy is knowing what literate people know, and the amount of traditional information people (even the literate ones) know is declining, then the list should simply shrink and change accordingly.

Hirsch's most ambitious claim is that universal literacy is equivalent to democracy. I believe that some kind of literacy may be necessary for real democracy (i.e., participatory democracy), but it is not sufficient. It is gross oversimplification to say that there are no factors except superficial cultural literacy operating in American society that contribute to inequality and undemocratic conditions. His main goal, Hirsch says, is full democratic participation in society by Americans, but he says he is opposed to trying to change culture on a large scale on the grounds that it can't be done (91). These two declarations are incompatible, as one can hardly imagine a bigger change in American culture than the elimination of poverty and social inferiority.

Hirsch builds his thesis of the equivalence of literacy and democracy on the very tenuous claim that mainstream culture is not ideologically biased. But if disadvantaged people only need to know what advantaged people know, and these two categories correspond to racial groups, it seems to follow that the needed knowledge in some sense belongs to and has origin in the group that is most successful. Where does their value system, their ideology, reside if not in the traditional lore of their culture?

Hirsch does not question the causal relationship involved; he assumes that what makes someone successful is the knowledge, cultural literacy, or not even the knowledge per se, but the sharedness of the knowledge. It seems more plausible that some other factors make people successful and that shared knowledge/lore/ideology are, at least partially, an effect rather than a cause; in other words, the dominant subculture, or class, of successful people—who are mainly white, conservative, and male— produces and reproduces whatever it likes, including tradition, lore, information, and so forth, which will promote and protect itself. And, since they control the means of production, including media technology, the traditions, lore, information, art, and so forth, those not in power will be marginalized and appropriated by the dominant class for its own ends. Nor does Hirsch explain why advantaged women, who are presumably as culturally literate as their male counterparts, are less successful than men. Of course, once the social structure is established, it is helpful for any outsider to "speak the language," but color, gender, sexuality, social skills, and connections will continue to loom as significant factors.

Hirsch uses the "fact" that high school students no longer share much knowledge and will, therefore, not be able to communicate with each other to attack current education theory, which he says produces a "fragmented," "shopping mall" curriculum from which students can freely pick a wide variety of frivolous and disconnected courses. It is not clear what the term "fragmented" means to Hirsch. A "pile" or "list" of information is essentially "fragmented" by one definition. Judging from the entire discussion, it can be inferred that Hirsch desires a conformist curriculum over a pluralistic curriculum in which students are allowed some freedom to pursue individual talents and interests, on the grounds that people can communicate better if their basic educations are identical.

Hirsch says that schools are teaching skills, not traditional American information needed for communication. But, in fact, most schools do require the same traditional courses with the same traditional textbooks full of the traditional information on his list. If students do not any longer know when the Civil War was fought, it isn't because they weren't "taught" the information and were "wasting" their time reading "essays on human feelings," or on how it "feels to be a daffodil," as some were fond of saying in the 1960s and 1970s; it is because, in the information age, such knowledge has been eclipsed by the bright, loud, and ubiquitous information of popular culture. They don't know when the Civil War was fought because they don't care. It is because they don't like school, don't like studying American history, and probably skipped class when it was assigned or dropped out of school altogether before the subject came up.

Hirsch completely sidesteps the widespread social problems that plague the education system, such as drugs, alcohol, pregnancy, sexually transmitted diseases, ennui, and violent crime. How could one who knows the national dropout rate at ninth grade suggest that the only problem of disadvantaged members of society is the lack of a prescribed list of traditional cultural information? Also, it is well established that people tend to learn and remember what they believe will be useful, not just what is put in front of them to mindlessly memorize. Students (young students) may well, as Hirsch claims, have a voracious appetite for memorization, but, most likely, though they may memorize with ease, if not relish, they need some incentive to do it.

A big problem with Hirsch's theory is that nowhere in his book does he define his basic concepts. He relies heavily on such words as "information," "understanding," and "knowledge," but never discusses what he means by them. He claims that children need to understand commonly used allusions to literature and mythology (30–31). He gives examples from the Bible, Mother Goose, and Greek mythology, but he doesn't say what he means by "understanding." Nowhere in the book does he say that people need to be able to analyze and evaluate information. But given the views of most of those who support Hirsch's program, it is fairly certain that he does not mean children should learn to regard both Zeus and God as mythological, or that they should study the nature and origins of mythology and religion at all.

It should be clarified that for Hirsch, "knowing" has very limited meaning—it has been reduced to mean vague recognition and association, the one value of which is that people who need to communicate with each other also vaguely "know" it. It seems reasonable to question how much benefit one gets out of "knowing" vaguely what *Moby Dick* is. Should one know that it is a nineteenth-century novel by Herman Melville, or that it is a story about a white whale named Moby Dick who is pursued by Captain Ahab, or that it is a movie starring Gregory Peck? None of this information compares to the incomparably rich experience of having read the novel, but according to Hirsch, one need not have read it or even been interested in it or any other novel or film or whales or biblical allusions in literature. One only needs a firing of neurotransmitters in the brain when the words "Moby Dick" are heard that means "that is a famous novel I never read."

This kind of knowing is deceptive and illusory because it tends to make people think they know something that they do not, in fact, know. Take the item "Karl Marx" on Hirsch's list. Most Americans, including teachers, do not hesitate to denounce Marx with vehement conviction. This value judgment is part of "knowing" Karl Marx in American culture, though most people have not read a single text by Marx. Given the already existing tendency in American culture to reduce knowledge of any subject to distorted slogans and generalizations, Hirsch's program would exacerbate this sort of ignorant opinionation.

For all of his insistence on the importance of the content being taught in school, Hirsch seems concerned not with the inherent value or truth of any of the information on his list or a context in which it might be meaningful for understanding something, but only with hazy knowing, or recognition, of some bits of raw data, whether fact, fiction, or superstition. His list includes some parables and proverbs that are a part of our cultural wisdom, but he says nothing about those insidious sayings and commonly held beliefs that are based on racial, sexual, or class prejudice, such as "women should be barefoot and pregnant" or "niggers are lazy" or "The only good Indian is a dead Indian." Is this not traditional lore? Do not many people, especially the white Anglo-Saxon Protestant good-old-boy males whose interests Hirsch adamantly denies he serves, use such cultural "wisdom" to establish the rapport needed for communication? In today's world, more than ever, it is important for survival to learn strategies for distinguishing accurate and useful information from disinformation and prejudice as well as to recognize the inherent biases and limitations of all information.

Hirsch says schools must teach "current mainstream culture," but his discussion and his list belie this edict. For example, one item on his list is "Star Wars," but there are two "Star Wars": the movie(s) and the Strategic Defense Initiative (SDI). Which does he mean? And if he listed both, what should we know about them? Common "knowledge" of SDI consists mostly of vague, if not erroneous, impressions and information. Part of the "knowledge" one is likely to have about SDI is prepackaged government-media opinion that is more political than scientific. Another part of SDI knowledge is awareness of its controversial nature. What, out of all this, does Hirsch want people to know? There is nothing in Hirsch's program that suggests a need to come to terms intelligently with this issue, nothing that suggests a need to acquire skills for learning, critiquing, communicating, and acting on important social issues such as SDI.

Also, current mainstream culture consists to a great extent of whatever mass media spectacles are being hyped to the public at any given moment. One month it is "Batman"; then it is "The Simpsons"; then it is "Teenage Mutant Ninja Turtles"; then it is *Jurassic Park*. These are not just movies and TV shows—they are orchestrated, packaged multimedia marketing extravaganzas. It never stops. Hirsch cannot publish revised editions of his cultural literacy dictionary fast enough to keep up if he wants to include the popular culture students all share.

Though Hirsch insists that his policy is to "represent," not "alter," "current American culture," he privileges scientific literacy by making it his only exception, because of its "growing importance in our lives" (136–137), that is, the need of nontechnical people to communicate with technical people and the need for both to participate in social decisions. Though the need unquestionably exists, Hirsch's logical positivist bias prevents him from understanding the position that equal attention must be given to social, psychological, philosophical, political, and artistic perspectives if everyone is to participate fully in social decisions. Apparently, Hirsch does not believe it is the duty of schools to teach students to be well-rounded human beings, but only to be able to do business with the technocrats.

Two of the most unfounded theses in Hirsch's theory are that no one lacks cognitive development and that critical thinking cannot be taught. The scientific evidence Hirsch offers to support these theses consists only of minimal citation of studies, from which he draws much larger conclusions than warranted. In later chapters, I will offer evidence for significant deficiencies in many students' cognitive development and arguments for the possibility of teaching critical thinking.

I agree with Hirsch that education must prepare students to change as the world changes. But education for change implies teaching thinking skills, problem-solving skills, the transferable skills Hirsch says cannot be taught. Once again, however, he draws unwarranted conclusions from select studies, and, of course, taken literally, Hirsch is saying that math, the scientific method, languages, logic, and many other subjects cannot be taught. It seems unthinkable that students could be educated for change by memorizing a list of disconnected data! In fact, all the studies I have seen on the problems of American society—in business and industry—point to a need for teaching critical thinking in school. I have never heard anyone but Hirsch say it can't be done.

Critical, abstract, and even creative thinking can to some extent be systematized scientifically and developed in those who follow suggested strategies, principles, and insights. There are many successful books and seminars on the subject, some of which I have followed in my own teaching with good results. That there is no rigid formula that guarantees predefined results does not imply that there is therefore nothing one can do. This is a relatively new discipline that is vital to the new paradigm I am presenting, and it should be nurtured by all progressive educators. It is simply not correct, as Hirsch implies, that schools are now emphasizing critical thinking. The subject is, at this point, for the most part, only being discussed; there is some classroom experimentation, but many recent studies affirm that American schools are not universally teaching critical thinking and also affirm the need.

The most valid point Hirsch makes is that people must have a certain foundation for developing reading and other social skills, in other words, for becoming effectively socialized. And he challenges those who disagree with his program for providing this foundation to think of something better. This book is offered as a response to this challenge. My approach is almost the opposite of Hirsh's—I say educators must look at culture to • see the dynamics outside of school that are forming and influencing students, in order that we may know who and what we are dealing with.

It is my counterproposal that the knowing necessary for reading and writing as well as individual and social development evolves naturally in the course of an education process that is designed to address the full range of individual and social needs in the contemporary world. This requires a restructuring of the education system—a new paradigm for education, not a reactionary amendment to the old one. Hirsch deplores fragmentation in the curriculum, but he himself represents the traditional mind-set, which is itself inherently fragmented and which created the problem he is attempting to solve with an alphabetized list of fragments of "culture." Hirsch is arguing that the solution to the literacy crisis, which for him is also the crisis of social inequality, is to intensify and regiment the static, mechanical information mode that currently pervades American education and call it a new solution.

I disagree with Hirsch's implication throughout the book that every issue is an either/or situation, for instance, either schools teach skills or they teach "facts." There is no reason why a healthy school system cannot offer students a common foundation of both cultural literacy and a wide range of useful physical and mental skills, in addition to individualized development. Inexplicably, near the end of his book, Hirsch reverses his position, admitting that "facts and skills are inseparable" and that proponents of both should "join forces" (133). It is this attitude that I appeal to in offering my concept of a more critical cultural literacy and a preliminary effort to define a context and a theoretical framework for it.

Whereas Hirsch's cultural literacy program is passive and rudimentary, my critical cultural literacy program is interactive and developmental. Whereas Hirsch's cultural literacy program neglects writing, my program emphasizes writing as an integral part of the critical cultural literacy necessary for independent thinking, an attribute much more suited to the exigencies of contemporary society than the noncritical conformity that Hirsh's program is likely to perpetuate.

At first I was planning to use the term "cultural literacy"; that was before it was "contaminated" by Hirsch. So I tried "critical cultural literacy" for a while. Then my daughter pointed out the inadequacies of that term, the primary one being that the denotations and connotations of "literacy" are too narrow and too established, making it a term unfit for a set of newer, broader concepts. We discussed it and thought about it for almost a year; then she suggested a term that I think I like. You be the judge. Maybe you can think of a better one.

"Critical cognitive activity" is the term I use. It will not be clearly understood until you have read my discussion of Vygotsky's theory of thought and language in chapter 5, in which the concept of "activity" (the English word probably being a poor substitute for the Russian word) figures prominantly. But you can see the idea of a mind participating in the world.

EDUCATION UNDER SIEGE

Education under Siege by Stanley Aronowitz and Henry Giroux (1985) identifies and critiques, from a radical point of view, the conservative, liberal, and radical forces in American education today. The authors are concerned about the many problems, fallacies, and contradictions in the current discourse about the crisis in education. Though many decry the failure of schools to train students for high-tech jobs, or even to keep students in school long enough to learn to read and write, and a few worry about students' lack of creative and critical thinking ability, Aronowitz and Giroux believe that so far, all the attempts at educational reform tend to be ineffectual, mostly technological solutions made by "experts" who reduce teachers to the status of implementers of reform. It is one of their central theses that teachers must play a central role in education reform.

Primarily, they say, conservative education reformists (most of whom are not, strictly speaking, themselves educators) focus on producing and maintaining the forms of knowledge which have already been legitimated as universal. Many progressive educators agree, differing from the conservatives mostly in their desire to make this "common culture" accessible to all. Radical educators, on the other hand, see this school culture as the culture of the ruling class designed to repress all other cultural expressions. Aronowitz and Giroux want to argue that none of these pedagogical positions enable "critical learning and social transformation" (1985, 139).

Though they think there have been many important contributions to education theory in the last several years, all have fallen short of developing an adequate theory of culture, schooling, and power that could produce a language of possibility for practical pedagogy. They focus most of their attention on critique of the conservative approach to education reform because it is currently the approach that is having the most success in implementing its designs. Basically, the new public philosophy celebrates economic and technocratic reason, which, for them, means that problems are being identified and defined incorrectly, and that erroneous solutions are being advocated (1985, 201).

Aronowitz and Giroux claim that the new conservative public philosophy abdicates its responsibility to create an education that will develop personally and politically emancipated citizens. They also argue that the ideological and political interests of those engineering the school reforms are antithetical to the notion that a central purpose of public education is the need to educate students to uphold the principles of a democratic society (24). They conclude that the dominant public philosophy, with its emphasis on privatized economic interests, embodies a very narrow view of learning and is a threat to the "politics of possibility" (206).

According to Aronowitz and Giroux, today's education debate is not about fulfilling the American dream of social equality; justice is not the goal of the neoconservative reformers, who are primarily concerned with the changing world economy. Schools are considered "producers of human capital." But the conservatives' strength is in their appropriation of all the issues, such as morality, family values, patriotism, and the good life, as well as the economy.

The conservative education agenda calls for a more rigorous science and math curriculum. "Their language of achievement, 'excellence,' 'discipline,' and 'goal orientation' really means vocational education or, in their most traditional mode, a return to the authoritarian classroom armed with the three R's curriculum" (2). Curriculum theory and the programs it has produced have been largely stripped of a "democratic vision" in order to function to educate students to be "obedient civil servants and skillful technicians" (142). "The conflation of education and training has become the emblem of the new era in higher schooling." The function of transmitting Western culture to the elite has been displaced by the function of technical training (170).

Taking this policy to task, even on its own terms, Aronowitz and Giroux argue that all the evidence suggests that technological change will result, indeed has already resulted, in the necessity for less and less specialized training, not more. People will need the general skills of logic, abstraction, and conceptualization, which will be invaluable for adapting to change (189).

They see a steady increase in anti-intellectualism in American life, which has always been present in American ideology, but which in our increasingly visual culture is increasing (48). A big problem in education today resulting from this anti-intellectualism is the trend toward deskilling teachers. This consists of the school administration presenting teachers with prepackaged materials, which are usually given to be objective, authoritative distillations of the knowledge of a discipline from only one point of view. This is similar to the way Thomas Kuhn describes science textbooks as presenting scientific research as a neat, logical, orderly process rather than the complex, political, and messy activity it really is.

The trend toward reducing the status of teachers is part of a larger cultural problem of intellectual and social labor becoming increasingly separated along with the increasingly oppressive management of daily life (24) and the growing objectification of human beings (31). Much of the prepackaged material in schools today attacks the teachers' role as intellectuals who are capable of assessing the needs of their students and designing appropriate lessons. This practice reduces teachers to "simply carrying out predetermined content and instructional procedures" (149).

Not only are teachers no longer required or even allowed to think for themselves under the current policies, but students are not taught to think. It is a very serious, if not insurmountable, problem when people lack the ability to think theoretically and conceptually, as the Frankfurt school is famous for noting. Their contention that our technologized, consumerized mass media culture industry created just such an effect has been borne out by recent research showing a tendency in children toward narrowing of perception and increasing difficulty in forming concepts and thinking abstractly, logically, and creatively. Aronowitz and Giroux say that the state of the American intellect may be so bad that the entire liberal tradition of critical thought is in peril, not just the more radical effort to encourage social action.

In addition to the big problem of functional illiteracy, there is a perhaps even bigger problem of historical and critical conceptual illiteracy, which produces the condition for the possibility of corporate control replacing democracy. Conceptual illiteracy—the inability to formulate ideas, to think independently and creatively—is due to the technicalization of education, but also to the mechanized American vision of the world. None of the education reform proposals, left or right, deal adequately, if at all, with the problem of a conceptually illiterate population (51, 64).

Literacy problems, in the ordinary sense, are much less serious than, and are probably even caused by, the problem that people cannot think through the complexities, subtleties, contradictions, and ambiguities of their own world. *"The degree to which mass audience culture has colonized the social space available to the ordinary person for reading, discussions, and critical thought must be counted as the major event of social history in our time"* (51, my emphasis).

Aronowitz and Giroux have observed a deep and widespread sense of gloom among college educators because of their awareness of the massive indifference toward critical thinking and the great difficulty if not futility involved in changing the situation. An optimistic response is that the current concern with literacy may provide an opportunity for changing the situation. In agreement with Douglas Kellner, Aronowitz and Giroux say that, despite the colonization of consciousness by the culture industry, learning is not totally determined—there are moments of resistance (51). They, at least in part, blame radical educators for the current situation in which conservatives dominate the debate over education. Conservative coalitions have formed around popular ideological issues while radical educators have neglected the concerns of people in their daily lives.

In their 1993 updated edition, *Education Still under Siege,* they expand this point noting that in the Reagan/Bush years, neoconservatives fully assumed the role of reforming education, of addressing the real social problems in a way that radicals did not. They have capitalized on popular emotions, worries, values, and fears to promote traditional values, especially family values, cultural uniformity, and punitive authoritarianism. In fact, the Reagan/Bush years saw increased student poverty, worsened teacher conditions, loss of school funding, and myriad other social problems, such as increased violent crime among school-age children. In September 1993, a study showed that fully half the adult population of the United States—90 million men and women, many of whom graduated from high school—cannot do the computations, reading, and writing necessary to hold a job. And the trend is worsening ("Washington Week in Review" 1993).

Leftist educators are in a "theoretical cul de sac" because they deny the possibility of finding power within the schools. They tend to ignore the reality of contradictions within the system that can be exploited; they overemphasize the way schools promote economic and cultural inequality while underemphasizing the way students resist, mediate, and accommodate the dominant practices. Consequently, Aronowitz and Giroux recommend the positive potential in the relationship of knowledge and power, not just the negative.

Power, they say, should be understood as both a positive and negative force—negative when it functions to reproduce the relations of domination, and positive when it functions to oppose and struggle, to refuse domination. "Hegemony—whether it takes place in the schools, the mass media, or the trade unions—must be fought for constantly in order to be maintained" (Aronowitz and Giroux 1985, 88, 89). It requires the constant structuring and controlling of consciousness which can never be complete and will always meet with resistance (71).

Schools are contested terrain. Schools, particularly colleges and universities, are battlegrounds on which the future is being fought for (52). They should be sites for struggling to develop a better, more democratic life. Curricula must be designed to give students an active and critical voice, the foundation for the skills needed in the modern world. Curriculum theory must relate knowledge and power; that is, it must analyze the politics behind all knowledge claims and the connection between schooling and cultural processes which produce and legitimate class, race, and gender attitudes.

Educators must define themselves and how they process experience. They must know how power is used to structure language to become a force for shaping people. They must argue for "critical literacy" as a necessity for cultural power. Teaching critical literacy means helping people learn how to analytically and critically read the texts of their experience. It means helping students to see themselves as socially produced, to some extent, so they can decide what they might want to change. It means questioning the instrumentalization and technicalization of American education (132).

Educators need to "rethink the nature and role of being a teacher" (160), to be "transformative political intellectuals," to see their social function as "mediators between the state and everyday life" (135). They must learn to treat students as critical agents, to "problematize knowledge, utilize dialogue, and make knowledge meaningful, critical, and ultimately emancipatory." Teachers must give students an active voice in their learning experience so they can develop a critical faculty that will serve them in day-to-day problem solving (37).

A new kind of teacher training is needed that will promote mastery of high culture but also popular culture, in order to relate to student experience. In fact, high culture should be seen as a part of popular culture, though so far most high schools and colleges do not consider popular culture worthy of legitimate academic study. Therefore, even when popular culture is taught, it can be difficult to convince students to take it seriously.

A new model of curriculum theory and practice must be developed that aims at the following objectives: "(1) an expanded notion of the political, (2) an attempt to link the languages of critique and possibility, (3) a discourse which views teachers as intellectuals, (4) and a reformation of the relation between theory and practice." In contrast to both liberal and conservative theories, the concept of the political should be expanded to mean "the entire way we organize social life, along with the power relations that inform its underlying social practices" (140).

An important problem that has not been widely acknowledged and one that pedagogical theory must face is the students' conditioned refusal to know or learn. Many students who reach college are severely blocked concerning certain ways of interrogating and critiquing experience. Over time, students have acquired an unconscious system of needs, thought, perception, and so on that cannot be altered by conscious efforts or even made conscious and that persist even after the conditions that created it are gone. Often ignorance is a certain way of *knowing*, which actively rejects particular knowledge, ideas, or themes. It is the result of curriculum policies, textbooks, and a variety of other factors in school and culture (Aronowitz and Giroux 1993, 7). Somehow they need to learn how not to be "imprisoned by the worst dimensions of their sedimented histories and experiences" (Aronowitz and Giroux 1985, 157). Radical educators must address the needs and desires of students, showing how alienating social structures produce repression and what can be done about it.

A key element of education must be the mastery of language; it is essential to developing the capacity to think conceptually and critically. Herein lies the link between English classes and the emancipatory goals of education. Aronowitz and Giroux are concerned about how the widespread technicalization process is producing a proliferation of composition programs and courses that are split off from literature. They disapprove of this split, arguing that it promotes writing as a technical skill rather than as an expressive and intellectual process that is vital in the development of critical thought. Studies show that the collective perception of English composition teachers today is that the decline in cognitive skills has reached nearly universal proportions.

Aronowitz and Giroux recommend using English composition courses to reverse the current trend toward literalness—the merging of thought with object that seems to have become the new universal of human consciousness—and to deconstruct the mass culture spectacle in which students are entranced; to wake them up out of their dreamlike trance in which media events such as TV shows and rock concerts are more real than any other part of their lives including (or especially) school. They argue, as I will in this book, that *"teachers must meet students on their own ground by intellectually analyzing the media and mass culture, and legitimating them in order to teach students to criticize and, perhaps, transcend them* (52). *A radical pedagogy must analyze, critique, and challenge the codes underlying the forms of signification found in the schools* (148). *It must 'deconstruct' the relations of daily school life in order to reveal the embedded ideology and 'structured silences' "* (146, my emphasis).

I agree with everything Aronowitz and Giroux say; in fact, I have let them convey these ideas for me because I was so surprised and pleased that I found so many of the ideas that I was in the process of writing about already in print and so well expressed. If that were all I had to say, I wouldn't bother now; it's already been said. But such an analysis and proposal is only the beginning. Every point they make must be taken up again and again by many educators and thinkers of all kinds coming from many points of view and areas of expertise in order to flesh out a new theory and practice for education and, correspondingly, for society. A few teachers who mean well simply can't effect the changes sketched by Aronowitz and Giroux. We are talking about a cultural revolution—a paradigm shift. Fortunately, *it has already begun.* It is part of my agenda to show that. One indicator is the huge flap over "political correctness," the now infamous PC. Many powerful opponents of the radical reform of education rant unceasingly that the good traditional form and content of education on which the success of our civilization rests and depends is being relentlessly destroyed by feminists, minorities, Marxists, and multicultural deviants of all types. In fact these so-called radicals hardly have gained a foothold and even lose ground quickly when there are funding problems or protest. But the over-reaction may be promising.

One of the hardest knots to untie in realizing this new vision of education is the tremendous influence that the traditional conservative power establishment has on education. American ideology essentially controls American education; there's not much difference between the inside and the outside of the education system ideologically, especially, I believe, at the primary and secondary levels where young minds are socialized and conditioned. What I am saying is that the schools by and large accommodate the status quo in society and are instructed by it. Therefore, to say, as Aronowitz and Giroux do, that "radical" teachers ought to go against the current system is to open a very large can of worms.

How is it that teachers are going to deviate from the norms with impunity, and how many teachers at the present time would have any idea what exactly to do, even if they agreed in principle with the radical agenda, given most teachers' intellectually, pedagogically, and politically weak training? Aronowitz and Giroux say, for example, that teachers must deconstruct the mass culture spectacle in which students are entranced. How many teachers at the present time have any idea what that means? Not many, I think. Aronowitz and Giroux don't explain this complex concept, and even if they had tried, it is really a set of concepts that takes a long time of study and thought and synthesis of ideas to understand, and certainly a long period of creative methodological experimentation to implement in the classroom.

What is "deconstruction"? What can it mean in relation to teaching? These questions alone are difficult to answer, and there are many possible answers, only of few of which have been explored so far. What is meant by "mass culture spectacle"? This is not a widely used concept. What does it mean to say students are "entranced" by mass culture? What cognitive, neurological, psychological knowledge is needed to understand this concept? These are all concepts that I am at great pains to discuss in this book—precisely because I know that not many people and not many teachers know what they mean or how valuable, if not absolutely essential, they are to the project of reforming education.

A huge problem that must be addressed is that a college-level teacher, even one with a low profile, can become persona non grata when word gets around about his or her "radical" ways. In most primary or secondary schools, I feel quite sure that the days of even a quietly radical teacher would be numbered. So if we are to take our vision seriously as more than just another pious dream about how the world ought to be, we have to confront very difficult questions and problems.

We have to realize that what we are attempting will not be easy, and may be impossible at this time. I think we ought to try. But one of the important differences between those of us who want a revolution in education and those who don't has to be that we know what we are up against and there are no easy answers, not even very many assumptions we can make. Those who want to cure the ills of society with bandaids on education and other social institutions do not perceive the ills the same way as do those who want revolution: this is the primary fact.

Establishment liberals and conservatives tend to see the same problems and then come up with different (sometimes only slightly different) solutions that are usually only modifications of the existing system, not structural or ideological changes based on a willingness to question their most basic and cherished assumptions about how the world is, how it should be, and how to get there from here. The warmly and widely received cultural literacy program of Hirsch attests to this fact—one simple solution to all the problems of education and society.

As my father used to say, you can't get there from here. Because "there" and "here" are fantasies, ideological constructs not very well lined up with much of the evidence we have at our disposal with which to interpret the world. Let us not make the same mistakes, though of course we will want to, because that is the way we have all been taught to think. That is where deconstruction comes in. I will discuss it in depth in a later chapter, but for now I will just say that it is a tool to help us identify and move away from ways of thinking that will only undermine, even destroy, our project. Our ideas of "there" and "here" will be constructs, too, but getting to first base, I think, consists of getting the best handle we can on reality, how things are. And the first principle underlying this project is to use deconstruction to help us be mindful that we will always be walking on thin ice. Anyone who thinks that part is easy has already fallen in, drowned, and frozen.

The fact that Hirsch's argument has been taken seriously by anyone is, to my way of thinking, a very strong sign that the thinking about education in our society is dangerously impoverished and misguided.

TOWARD CRITICAL COGNITIVE ACTIVITY

In an attempt to address this crisis of cultural illiteracy as defined and evaluated by Aronowitz and Giroux, I will now attempt to chart a path toward a new pedagogical theory that will enable the production of emancipatory education.

In chapter 2, I discuss the aspects of contemporary American culture that are most instrumental in shaping Americans today. Education, obviously, does not operate in a vacuum, and therefore it is necessary to consider as much as possible, as overwhelming as the task might seem, the factors impinging on the matter of teaching—one of the most important of which is culture. Not only is culture important because it has, to a great extent, determined the individual, whom we must know a great deal about if we are to teach effectively, but culture is important because it is the environment in which we educators are preparing students to cope. Through the studies of a variety of anthropologists, media experts, and social scientists, I show Americans' noncritical vulnerability to media domination and their deficiencies in perceiving, analyzing, and coping with today's complex problems. My emphasis is on electronic media technology, particularly TV—how it functions in society and its effects on individuals, society, and literacy.

Chapter 3 discusses the search for a new paradigm for education, which is at the same time a new paradigm for society in general. I show that in a variety of disciplines, a few of which I discuss, new paradigms for thinking are evolving, opening up new frontiers. Physics and chaos theory provide us with new models of basic reality. Neurology provides us with new models of the brain and mental processes. Cognitive psychology provides us with new models of human behavior and learning. All of these cutting-edge theories can point the way and offer valuable insights and knowledge.

In chapter 4, I discuss deconstructive thinking as the basis for the new paradigm. It is among the theorists labeled poststructuralists, especially the deconstructionist Jacques Derrida, that I find the critiques and models of thought and culture appropriate for establishing cultural and critical literacy. I discuss deconstruction in general and how it can provide an approach to the crisis in education.

To provide a theoretical framework for the new paradigm, I present the theory of L. S. Vygotsky in chapter 5. An educator and cognitive psychologist, Vygotsky shows us in his theory of the dynamic dialectical processes and developmental stages of thought and language that the individual and society are inseparable and that the higher mental functions that are essential for full maturity of both individual and society are internalized social relations dependent on language. I then attempt to show how Vygotsky's theory can help educators and teachers better understand the social and educational problems that I have tried to identify and how it can help them conceptualize "critical cognitive activity" and the central roles of thinking, writing, and social problem solving in education under the new paradigm. Finally, in the appendix, I discuss pedagogical methods, principles, and resources that can be used in teaching critical cognitive activity.

Most of my sources in this study probably do not know of each other, nor, in many cases, would they appreciate or agree with each other. But I see their interconnectedness and complimentarity and believe that it is very worthwhile to formulate a more or less coherent "big picture" made up of as many diverse perspectives as possible, in the style proposed in *Against Method* by Paul Feyerabend. He says that "anything goes." He means that in problem solving people should not be restricted to only one structure of reality, but should take from many theories and cultures. This "Dada" method, as he called it, is taking material at hand and creatively making what is needed to challenge existing authority; it is similar to the montage method of postmodern theory, which invokes a pastiche of images that provoke thought and new connections, as opposed to the rationalist model of a linear logical totality. Only in this way can we begin to appreciate the complexity of our society, to see new, distinct patterns emerging from disparate data and views, and to engage in creative problem solving.

I apologize for the gender and ethnic imbalance of my bibliography. Using mostly white male authors to make my argument tends to undermine my argument, but most of them are antiestablishment and some are actively anti-elitist, antisexist and antiracist. However, I should have made more of an effort to find more female and nonwhite sources; they are plentiful but, of course, usually less visible. I am currently working on this vital dimension and hope that I will have the opportunity to publish a second, improved edition of this text.

My method is to sketch, sometimes in considerable detail, studies and arguments from the vast intellectual constellation that directly inform or indirectly shed light on my project. I present a montage, if you will, of provocative connections in combination with a linear and recursive argument in an effort to explore heretofore untapped resources in my quest for a new pedagogical paradigm.

What I mainly hope to show is that Americans are in precisely the grave danger George Orwell (1949) depicted in *Nineteen Eighty-Four*, because they are losing the ability to think, cope, and develop creatively and effectively, and they do not know they are losing it. I submit that teaching critical cognitive activity is the key to reversing this situation, providing the condition of the possibility for creative change.

II

Contemporary American Culture: Values, Media, and Technology

"You're a closed circuit, baby."

—Laurie Anderson*

Critical cognitive activity entails analyzing, evaluating, and challenging social values. The investigation of the history and forces behind these values leads to the study of media and technology—especially, today, the electronic media—particularly television. This chapter presents an overview of contemporary American values followed by a discussion of the influences of mass media and technology in general. The focus is on television as the strongest technological force in, and probably the best metaphor of, American culture. My thesis is that the teacher of critical cognitive activity must address the student's naivete concerning technology, mass media, and culture by teaching critical analysis of and problem-solving strategies for dealing with dominant cultural forces.

Social scientist Daniel Yankelovitch (1981) abstracted a portrait of the American ethos in 1981, compared it to the ethos of the fifties, and made speculations and predictions about the future.

*From "Closed Circuits" by Laurie Anderson. © 1984 Difficult Music.

Photograph by Barbara Kruger, 1982. Used by permission.

In his book *New Rules*, the result of thirty years of scientific social research on American values, he claims that eighties' values were characterized by a somewhat immature desire for self-fulfillment clumsily wedded to yesterday's values of self-denial and duty and predicated on unrealistic notions of self and society.

Thirty years of national surveys by Yankelovitch, Skelly, and White, show that by the outset of the 1980s 80 percent or so of adult Americans had changed their values, touched by the great shifts in culture. Their studies show that a majority of around 83 percent felt some need for a creative lifestyle and affluence. About 17 percent were extremely committed to self-fulfillment—Yankelovitch calls these "strong-formers"—and the rest struggle in the "weak form" of the self-fulfillment predicament; their inner lives are rarely subject to upheaval; they retain many traditional values, including a moderate commitment to the old self-denial rules; but they try to achieve greater freedom, choice, and flexibility in their lives (1981, 91).

A new social ethic was taking shape; Yankelovitch (1981) calls it an "ethic of commitment. . . . Without a social ethic there is no assurance that the adaptive side of the self-fulfillment search will triumph. In our demand for greater fulfillment in a time of economic turbulence, we have set in motion forces that can lead either to a higher stage of civilization or to disaster. Will we achieve a synthesis between traditional commitments and new forms of fulfillment to create a new direction for our society? Or will we indeed end up with the worse of two worlds?" (12).

From the 1950s to the late 1960s, Americans believed that the present was better than the past and that the future would be even better, but there was a historic shift away from optimism to bleakness in the late 1970s characterized by a sharp decline in trust of government and other institutions and pessimism about personal economic prospects as well as America's economic future.

After *New Rules* was published, there was a strong swing back to optimism orchestrated by the media at the hands of Big Business and government, spearheaded by the 1984 Reagan "feel-good-again" reelection campaign. At this writing, though there have been ups and downs, and the rejection of the Reagan-Bush regime may signal a growing desire to cope more realistically with problems, there is still a somewhat myopic Disneyesque mood thoughout the United States. College students (and their parents) tend to think only of money, commodities, and entertainment, and technological advancement is controlled by the military-industrial-corporate complex for short-term profits rather than used for global needs in a world where one-fifth of the world population live in dire poverty (Durning 1992, 27). The media propaganda blitz of the Reagan/Bush years has been incredibly effective in repressing truth and shaping mainstream Americans' values into a solid, simple equation of God = Capitalism = Patriotism: a holy trinity, if you will.

Most people seem to believe that America offers great rewards in an open contest with clear rules. The nation's motivating force for individual achievement is this opportunity to acquire social status, money, recognition, and so forth (Yankelovitch 1981, 141). "For the overwhelming majority of all Americans, an important part of living the good life simply means 'more' " (176).

The study also concludes that, overall, Americans do not reject the idea of hierarchical social class and care very little about reducing income inequality. The majority do not want any redistribution that seems to take away the earnings of the successful. "The national psychology holds that those who play the game according to the rules (. . . luck, hard work, and good connections), are entitled to their success, and should be able to reenvest liberally what they get" (141).

America's psychology of affluence is characterized by (1) expecting a high material standard of life at no sacrifice to the environment, social programs, and so on, (2) believing oneself to be entitled to everything, (3) believing that the economy is a "Big Mother" whom one can take for granted, and (4) believing that duty to self supersedes duty to others. Many do not yet realize that this psychology is not realistic, does not reflect reality. "The unprepared mind plays tricks on itself," says Yankelovitch—it imagines that everything will somehow work out. Americans have not yet reconciled themselves to the new unpleasant reality that America is not as affluent as it once was, that there have been important economic changes in America and throughout the world. People have not faced up to the necessity of finding strategies for coping based on lowered economic expectations. And they are not likely to as long as denial, not adapting, is the pervasive strategy currently being hard-sold by the establishment. Studies show that, as people feel the contradiction between economic reality and received dogma, they have become less tolerant of social programs, environmental priorities, and foreign "enemies"; bigotry, sexism, and xenophobia are on the rise again in an effort to preserve the status quo (188–190). Indeed, since *New Rules* was written, these traits have persisted, even worsened, probably more than anyone's predictions.

Many critics of modern industrial society condemn it for having tendencies that make it impossible for people to fully realize themselves as human beings. Until the 1970s most Americans soundly rejected this criticism. But in the 1970s they began to take it seriously, as they desired to change their "getting/giving contract" with society. Throughout most of this century, Americans believed that self-denial, sacrifice, obeying the rules, and subservience to the institution made sense. But doubts set in, and by 1980, 70 to 80 percent of Americans believed that the old getting/giving contract needlessly restricted the individual while advancing the power of government, business, and religion, which use their power to enhance their own interests at the expense of the public (Yankelovitch 1981, 228–231).

Millions of "life experiments" had the power to make a cultural revolution, to create a new shared meaning. The old shared meaning said that poverty is not destiny and political freedom can coexist with, even enhance, material well-being. The new shared meaning insists that the personal freedom to shape one's life can coexist with, even civilize, the instrumentalism of modern technological society. But to Yankelovitch (1981) this view is extremely naive; for example, he cites cultural historian William Irwin Thomson, who says, "The major drift of advanced industrial society . . . is toward an authoritarian system." He sees "the whole culture spinning downward to darkness in a tightening spiral" (228). One problem that Yankelovitch sees is the deeply rooted assumption of a culture-free "self," which should be identified and extirpated, for there is much harm to society and the individual in the failure to see that self and culture are deeply interconnected. I will discuss this later.

Another problem is a misunderstanding of the concept of freedom; for clarification Yankelovitch uses Hannah Arendt's notion that freedom is different from liberation. Liberation is a necessary precondition for freedom, but it is what people do with their liberty that determines whether they are free or not. Liberation restores lost rights, but freedom is people helping shape the course of their own society. "If the great choices that determine our destiny are made for us by others—by elites, by technicians, by elected officials—then we are not free. . . . If in searching for self-fulfillment the citizens of a 'free country' like America pay attention only to the private self, they are not free" (Yankelovitch 1981, 221, 222). Today the ubiquitous and univocal voice of advertising has appropriated the concept of freedom as well as that of patriotism, reducing them to the choice of which American-made product to charge on one's VISA card.

Yankelovitch (1981) suggests that the psychology of affluence is quite inappropriate for survival in today's world, though it thrives with a vengeance. He warns that "the disparity between entitlement claims and resources looms so large that a self-fulfillment strategy based on a more-of-everything premise is simply futile. . . . The success of this new cultural revolution hinges on how skillfully the seekers of self-fulfillment can, in the economic conditions of our era, now discard the most harmful and obsolete features of their life experiments and simultaneously encourage the healthy and adaptive features to come to the fore" (233–234).

There is a battle waging right now over the "ethical status of desire and the question of what moral meaning to assign to needs and wants" (249). The 1950s ethic, which is weaker now, but still powerful and regaining strength under the aegis of "making America great again," is the Protestant work ethic of self-denial, hard work, and virtuous profit. In contrast is the self-fulfillment ethic. Yankelovitch says we need a new social ethic that neither suppresses nor condones desires indiscriminately, an ethic of commitment, which is self-fulfillment without ever-increasing wealth or wasteful depletion of resources. What is good for the individual should be good for society. An ethic of commitment will "shift the axis away from the self (either self-denial or self-fulfillment) toward connectedness with the world"

(250), toward "understanding that the resolution of our private predicaments will also shape the civilization in which we live, and conversely, that any new social ethic will decisively redefine the individual search for fulfillment" (12–13).

We need new rules—we are disoriented without a workable social ethic. "Sooner or later the psychology of affluence will be forced to yield to a social ethic better suited to the new economic realities. But before it does we can expect a period of tense and bitter political conflict" (213). Yankelovitch predicted the reduction in the American standard of living which has indeed come to pass. He said the powerful would become more powerful—they have—the weak, more weak—and they have. He said there would be more racial strife, unemployment, suffering, divisiveness, regional conflict, and there has been. Yankelovitch anticipated "intense social conflict, economic stress and confusion in signals" because "the public is still mired in unrealistic expectations and still entranced by the seductions of duty to self. The voices that interpret to us the meaning of changes in the world—our political leadership, the mass media—come across muffled and confused" (261).

Yankelovitch predicted that through the 1980s, at least, the struggle between the haves and have-nots would increase as part of society is protected against inflation and part not. There would be new conflicts, such as those pitting young against old. There would be more divisive battles on abortion, school prayer, sex education, criminal justice, the death penalty, censorship, and civil rights. And "eventually we will have to face the race of rot in our institutions and infrastructure—the inability of our schools to teach" (261).

Looking back at the eighties from the early nineties, one can see clearly that we are in the throes of these conflicts with no end in sight. In fact, there is a dangerous development that Yankelovitch did not foresee, the production of a simulacrum of the ethic of commitment produced by advertising and paid for by the powerful to disguise business as usual. "Peace-shield" (a.k.a. Star Wars) technology and military aggression feed the economy in the name of a new age of war prevention and democratic freedom fighting. Indeed, the 1991 Gulf War was fought for "peace," "fairness," a "New World Order."

A book read by many more people than *New Rules* is the heavily promoted series of best-sellers, *Megatrends,* by John Naisbitt (1982). This book I perceive to be more harmonious with the general mood of society: admitting a few problems, but undermining the admission with confident optimism about the future.

Typical of the contemporary American mind-set, Naisbitt is glib and noncritical, never going to any depth in his analyses, and mistaking "potentiality" for "inevitability." Naisbitt says that American society is now in a "time of parentheses," the time between eras, a time of change and questioning (1982, 279). As a society, we have to "reconceptualize what we are up to" (82). He believes that America has begun this reconceptualization and that long-range realistic planning will promote peace and a safe environment as we become a global economy with all major countries. He sees a healthy trend toward a reformed attitude in business and business school education, which have been widely criticized for being obsessed with short-term profit.

Yet other critics show how the vast majority of America's research and development money goes for defense spending of highly questionable value and minor changes and improvements of commodities for the purpose of competition. And as cultural anthropologist Marvin Harris says in his book *America Now: The Anthropology of a Changing Culture* (1981), government is increasingly wasteful and inefficient and American business uses advertising propaganda to persuade consumers that U.S. products are better rather than actually trying to improve quality. He argues that from a holistic perspective, the main cause of inflation is decrease in the quality of goods and services due to inefficient bureaucracies and oligopolies run by alienated and desensitized workers. More recent studies on American business have confirmed these conclusions.

Naisbitt (1982) predicts that, more and more, people will be reconceptualizing their roles and creating a shared vision in a participatory manner, bottom up—America is becoming decentralized—and that the conformity of mass society is a "thing of the past." We are, he says, abandoning the hierarchical structure in favor of networking, largely because of the electronics industry, which will be the biggest industry ever created. Though he acknowledges that "high tech" must be balanced with "high touch" and that technology will never liberate us from personal discipline and responsibility, he is confident that technology will "extend and enhance our mental ability" as long as we "balance the human element." But Harris (1981) says that as technology goes up, quality of life goes down, that in the computer age people are becoming increasingly formal, impersonal, and inefficient, locked into a rigid structure, alienated by decrease in human interaction in the workplace.

Contrary to Naisbitt, Harris demystifies the "electronic cottage" and argues that "what was once a decentralized manufacturing society has become a centralized service and information-processing society" (1981, 166). Moreover, automation reduces the number and quality of jobs; it means "less to know and less to think" (52–53). Harris, like Yankelovitch, sees increased racism, sexism, homophobia, problems in education and government, and so on, but his solution rests not so much on a new ethical paradigm as on a new intellectual paradigm, a holistic approach to the problems of American society: "America's problems cannot be understood piecemeal" (140); people must see the interconnectedness of all the parts and changes of culture.

He thinks that by and large, Americans do not understand problems because there is little public discussion of their root causes. This ignorance may make matters worse, as it leads to such powerful and popular movements as right-wing evangelism, which Harris considers to be a search for solutions to social and economic, not spiritual, problems.

Another of the many voices more critical but less heard than Naisbitt is social analyst Colin Norman. In his book *The God That Limps: Science and Technology in the Eighties* (1981), Norman argues, as Harris does, that the trend is not toward conservatism and efficient use of resources nor toward participatory democracy, though more public participation is needed in technological decisions and government action. He contends that nothing short of an overhaul of government priorities is necessary for effective energy technology. But most people don't know how new technology is developed and applied, even though these forces are key factors in shaping society and, at present, are not being directed toward solving world problems. The two biggest new technologies, microelectronics and biotechnology, can help solve worldwide problems or cause serious problems; in any case, they will alter production, jobs, and life in general.

The teacher of critical cognitive activity must know and expose students to these and other economic and social, national and global problems as well as the values that accompany them, the trends they are taking, and various viewpoints in analyzing them. This is an uphill battle in a society where military superiority and economic interests are the overriding concern, and students tend to be apathetic if not hostile toward any attempts to teach them anything that doesn't directly translate into financial success. Twenty years ago students and the general public were much more interested than they are now in politics and social issues. I can attest to that from my own teaching experience. Now, America, including most college students, has a general preoccupation with business and economics. In 1990 74 percent of Americans entering college said it was essential to be well off financially, compared with only 44 percent in 1967. Conversely, in 1990, only 43 percent thought it necessary to develop a meaningful philosophy of life compared with 83 percent in 1967 (Durning 1992, 34). Greatly exacerbating this business-mindedness is the consumerist mind-set that is created and reinforced by the messages that bombard everyone night and day through mass media, particularly TV. One sees statistics such as these that support the point: by the early eighties the United States had only about 6 percent of the world's population, but consumed around a third of the world's energy and produced over half of the world's advertising (Reis and Trout 1981, 11) at a cost of around 68 billion dollars per year (Bagdikian 1983, 189). In 1990, $500 per person were spent on advertising in the United States compared with $200 in 1950, and global spending rose to over $250 billion (Durning 1992, 120).

Consumerism, defined as the possession and use of more and more goods as the main cultural aim and way to success and happiness, was born in the United States, but now is rapidly spreading throughout the world creating a global culture. While western Europe and Japan are close behind (32), the United States still leads with over 35,000 shopping malls (130) headed by the Mall of America, the largest mall and amusement park located in Bloomington, Minnesota—an apt symbol for the

United States, which Durning says is remaking itself in the image of the mall (7). And, there is growing consumerism in more and more underdeveloped countries, such as India, Turkey, Indonesia, and Mexico with sharply increasing numbers of cars, televisions, shopping malls, appliances, and fashion items (35).

Durning, in his Worldwatch Institute study of the consumer society and the future, *How Much Is Enough?*, shows the high costs of consumerism. He argues with statistics that the consumer class, who he identifies as the richest 20 percent of the world population, around 1.1 billion people taking 64 percent of the world income, is responsible for most of the damage people are doing to the environment; for example, the emission of carbon dioxide into the atmosphere from use of fossil fuels: those in the poor class, about 1.1 billion people earning less than $700 per year, release about one-tenth ton per year per person, the middle income class, about 3.3 billion people earning between $700 and $7500 per year per person, about one-half ton, and the consumer class three and one-half tons—the richest one-tenth of Americans alone release eleven tons per person per year (27). There are similarly staggering statistics for consumption of all other resources. In short, high consumption means high impact on the environment. The richer people are, the more ecologically damaging products they buy and the more they waste resources through excessive packaging, planned obsolescence, overeating, and so forth.

In addition to ecological damage, consumerism appears, ironically, to have an adverse effect on quality of life. Global consumerism, led by the United States, is encouraging people all over the world to become more uniform and passive and to become less interested in their own culture, family, friends, and community. People tend to become obsessed with consuming and always imagine they would be happier if they had more, though studies show that there is little difference in the levels of happiness reported in very rich and very poor countries (39). And, of course, the wisdom of most, if not all, societies says that the elements of a happy life are social relations, work, and leisure, not consuming.

Durning doesn't discuss another important dimension of the consumer society: all those millions, maybe billions, who are consuming *images*, the messages of consumerism. Those people I call "virtual consumers"—they vicariously participate in global culture and dream of the day when they, too, will have full membership in the consumer society. Over one-half the world population has access to TV, according to Durning (127), so this group of virtual consumers growing daily is already larger than the consumer class. I have seen many examples of this myself; for instance, in a Turkish village where a family clusters around their only appliance, an old black and white TV, in a one-room dirt floor cottage with no toilet or running water watching "Dynasty."

Like Yankelovitch, Durning sees a need for a fundamental change in the American ethos. Similar to Yankelovitch's ethic of commitment is Durning's vision of the transformation of the consumer culture to a "culture of permanence" in which people consciously choose a lifestyle that is good for the environment while improving their standard of life (137). Voluntary simplicity, or what is now often called "green consumerism" (124) is a social movement committed to rejecting consumerism with a long history which has never been more than marginally successful (140). But now it must succeed, says Durning and others, and, happily, there are some indications that it is a growing movement. Durning cites the success in the United States of efforts to decrease smoking and a 1992 public opinion poll showing a move away from consumerism toward environmental protection (148). Also on an optimistic note, Durning points out that consumerism doesn't have deep cultural roots and that one isn't giving up anything of lasting value. But the paradigm of thought which produced consumerism has deep roots indeed. Therefore, nothing short of a new paradigm will do.

Exacerbating the problems of rampant consumerism in the United States is the growing gap between rich and poor predicted by Yankelovitch. Inequality in pay has dramatically worsened. In 1980 the top 4 percent of Americans earned in wages and salaries as much as the bottom 51 percent, compared with the bottom 39 percent in 1959 (Sklar 1993). In 1980 the average salary of a top executive of a large corporation was as much as the salary of forty-two factory workers, compared to 104 in 1991 (in Japan it's eighteen). The top 1 percent of American families have more money than the bottom 90 percent. In 1989 that amounted to 38 percent of total net worth in the United States. The top fifth had 84 percent of the wealth. Concentration of wealth is worse than anytime since 1929. Moreover, minimum wage has lost nearly 25 percent of its value since 1970 (Sklar 1993). Every day dozens of children die of poverty if not gunwounds in the United States (Sklar 1993), while we all are exhorted some 3000 times each day to consume more at all costs (Durning 1992, 118).

Positioning: The Battle for Your Mind, by advertising executives Al Reis and Jack Trout (1981), presents the consumerist worldview. They say that because of the vast amount of information that bombards the minds of people in our society, people are "overcommunicated"; they suffer sensory overload, rejecting much of the information and accepting mostly that which matches their prior knowledge and experience. The brain cannot function normally; therefore, the only defense is an oversimplified mind (6). "In our overcommunicated society," they say, "the human mind is a totally inadequate container" (35). Therefore, most people make up their minds and then find the facts to verify their opinion, or, even more commonly, they accept the opinion of the nearest "expert" so that they do not have to bother with the facts at all. This analysis will be discussed in detail in chapter 3.

Reis and Trout (1981) do not want to change people; they admittedly analyze people in order to exploit them, and they have concluded that the best approach in an overcommunicated society is the "oversimplified message." They claim, "You have to sharpen your message to cut into the mind. You have to jettison the ambiguities, and then simplify it some more if you want to make a long-lasting impression" (8). "Confusion is the enemy. Simplicity is the holy grail" (173). Select words that trigger the meanings you want. Selecting the right name for your product is especially important. The name is like the point of a knife; it opens up the mind to let the message penetrate (127).

One has only to look around in our bumper-sticker world to see verification of their analysis: It's Morning in America, It's Miller Time, It's Ford Country, It's the Pepsi Generation, Coke is it, Just do it. Obviously, if one's goal is short-term profit,

Photograph by Barbara Kruger, 1987. Used by permission.

not the long-term well-being of humanity, whatever works is fine. All's fair in the world of sales. As Reis and Trout (1981) put it, "It just happens to be the way things are. To be successful in this overcommunicated society of ours, you have to play the game by the rules that society sets. Not your own" (84–85). This cynical "I-didn't-make-the-rules / let's-play-hardball / dog-eat-dog / good-guys-finish-last" philosophy seems to be thriving in today's world of competitive "free" enterprise. This is the fare on which most of our students are raised, fare that is implicit in the pop ideology they uncritically parrot.

The serious problem here is, of course, that the world *is* complex and ambiguous, despite fantasies to the contrary and the inconveniences that the truth causes. Teachers of critical cognitive activity must take the responsibility for expanding students' (and by extension the public's) concepts of reality beyond the Walt Disney fantasy. The tactics of advertising have been institutionalized throughout society—through reductionism, glib truisms, the quick fix, denial, and tell-them-what-they-want-to-hear. This is where our students are "coming from."

Consumerism depends on mass electronic media for its power. And the largest, most powerful political and social force in the world is TV and radio. Says Tony Schwartz in *Media: The Second God* (1981), it is necessary to study how electronic media affect us; the effect is much different from the effect of print. Schwartz (19) says, "Only if we analyze some of the consequences of the shift from a print-dominated communication system to an electronic media–dominated system can we better solve the economic, social, political, and educational problems of the postliterate age. Such an analysis must begin with an examination of the differences between the print medium and the electronic media" (15). The shift from print to electronic media is now dominant and has already restructured the world.

Schwartz (1981) and others argue that the need to read and write is not as great as it was before the electronic age. He says that one does not have to read to learn and experience via electronic media, but he, like many other media experts, isn't considering the use of print in cognitive development or computer communication, nor is he acknowledging the questionable nature of the "knowledge" gained from TV and radio. It is arguable that only through print—reading and writing—combined with other media can one fully develop intellectually. This will be discussed later.

Certainly teachers need to understand how the media have made the mastery of reading and writing less urgent to the child. As Schwartz (1981) points out, the role of the school should no longer be to organize the distribution of information, but to teach students how to handle the vast amount of information available; that is, to teach students to think and to utilize TV, radio, print, and all forms of communication as tools. It seems that few teachers take this approach, and consequently, most students are uninterested in school.

Schwartz (1981) thinks it is very important for people to be aware of the tremendous power of the media to address social problems. We must consider the consequences of "so much media power in the hands of a group that is determined to affect moral, ethical, and political standards for the rest of the country. The original alliance between religion and radio may turn out to be one of the most powerful in history, an alliance between the first and second gods" (137). This phenomenon is fully explored by communication experts Flo Conway and Jim Siegelman in their *Holy Terror: The Fundamentalist War on America's Freedoms in Religion, Politics, and Our Private Lives* (1984). They say that the "electronic church" has become a "fixed feature of mass culture" that has brought a new style of politics into vogue: "the exploitation of religion as the vehicle for a larger social and political movement, a drive for power, not only at the national level, but in every domain of public concern, in the most intimate areas of our private lives, and in the volatile arena of world affairs." They call this "broad program of intimidation, manipulation, and control in the name of religion . . . *Holy Terror*" (4).

Though his case is understated and at some points unduly optimistic, Schwartz has the critical acuity to postulate the following: "The media have encouraged in us a growing preference for the new constructed reality. So overpowering is our involvement with electronic media generally that a face-to-face encounter may seem unreal in relation to our electronic communication reality" (1981, 50). He admits that developments in electronic media could go either way; they could supplement interpersonal interactions, or replace them.

Though most people seem to see TV as a largely positive social force with little or no harm in it, I will build on Schwartz's warnings and join the small but growing minority who believe they have evidence that TV has some very seriously harmful effects on individuals and society. For example, Marie Winn's *The Plug-In Drug* (1985) is compelling with its plethora of evidence of the negative effects of heavy TV watching, that is, the way America watches. Information, theories, and critiques warning us of the dangers of TV are plentiful and accessible, yet things stay the same or get worse. Winn's hard evidence and representative anecdotes alone should be enough to make any parent take an ax to the family TV set.

To start with, consider a few statistics: at least 95 percent of American households have one or more TV sets, which have been turned on an average of seven hours per day since 1984 (Winn 1985, x; Durning 1992, 125). Preschool children in America spend over one-third of their waking hours watching TV (Winn 1985, 4). Juvenile crime increased 1600 percent between 1952 and 1972—the years of the first TV generation. Between 1952 and 1974 violence on TV increased 90 percent (98). These and other statistics make a pattern which unmistakably implicate TV as a seriously negative force in American society.

On a TV newscast in September 1993, it was reported that teenagers see 14,000 sexual encounters per year in the media and that in 1992 teen pregnancies soared to one million. An eighteen-year-old has seen 18,000 simulated murders (and some real ones) on TV, and though there have been over 3,000 studies on TV violence since the 1950s, providing overwhelming evidence that TV contributes to aggressive behavior including murder, the trend continues (Cannon 1993). To cite one example, in Texas, juvenile violent crime more than doubled in the five years between 1988 and 1992, from 3,200 to 7,200 (Phillips 1993).

Winn (1985) believes that TV harms perception, language development, imagination, creativity, and relationships. Studies show that heavy TV watchers think the real world is like the TV world, education notwithstanding. For example, they believe their chances of being murdered are much greater than they really are (although the probability *is* rising—due to self-fulfilling prophesy, perhaps?), making them more paranoid, more likely to want a gun in the house, and more likely to support tougher crime-fighting policies though not, apparently, more likely to support the search for root causes and realistic solutions. Furthermore, "we cannot use our own imaginations to invest the people and events portrayed on TV with the personal meanings that would help us understand and resolve relationships and conflicts in our own life; we are under the power of the imaginations of the show's creators" (61).

The upshot of these effects of TV is a public whose psychologies and politics are shaped not by the way the world is, but by the way TV simulates it. Ben Bagdikian, in his book *The Media Monopoly* (1983), points out that children see more than 350,000 commercials by age seventeen, which do incalculable psychological and intellectual damage as the "propaganda arm of the American culture" (185–187). The figure was about the same in 1992 (Durning 1992, 128).

Winn's most serious accusation, however, is that heavy TV watching is very destructive to child development. She claims that it retards the development of children's minds and bodies to be watching TV during the second and third years, the very years when toddlers begin to assert their independence. Many parents begin putting kids in front of the TV at this stage for their own convenience. It is a narcotic for parents to give their children. "Just as they are beginning to emerge from their infant helplessness, they are lured back into passivity by the enticement of the television set" (Winn 1985, 173). Winn charges that parents have drifted back into a destructive style of child rearing, and claims that avoiding a child's needs with TV is similar to the beating and drugging of yesteryear. "Perhaps it was children's unprecedented complicity in their own pacification by television that allowed parents to employ it so relentlessly and so openly" (158). All in all, Winn believes that TV has a very negative effect on family life, alienating members from each other. Being in the same room together watching TV is not being together; it does not take the place of real interactions such as playing games or talking, which are necessary for bonding, socialization, emotional development, and learning.

A study on the relationship of TV and language development suggests that "serious diminution of verbal abilities has occurred among those children who grew up watching great quantities of television" (Winn 1985, 50). This may be due to understimulation of the left hemisphere of the brain and overstimulation of the right. Without a doubt, many aspects of brain anatomy and chemistry are altered by the stimulations received during developmental stages. And a sensory-deprived environment definitely leads to retardation (51–52). Heavy TV watching deprives children of the sensory experiences they need in order to develop properly. Watching television is a passive activity, and children need to interact with real people and their real environment. TV robs children of valuable interactions with their parents, verbal interactions, and playtime with other children, making them more dependent and less verbal (7).

Many people believe that TV programs such as "Sesame Street" make up for the loss of more traditional activities, such as reading, playing, being with the family. But a study of "Sesame Street" showed that the program did not contribute to children's development and demonstrably hindered development in disadvantaged children (Winn 1985, 37). All the evidence suggests that reading, an interactive event, cannot be replaced with TV watching, a passive activity. Moreover, there is an inverse correlation between SAT scores and TV habits. And in general, high scores on sections of the test requiring advanced reasoning skills are lower than they used to be (84).

The National Assessment of Educational Progress (NAEP) project showed a steady decline in academic skills at all grade levels during the 1970s and 1980s, including a significant decrease in inferential reasoning ability, a key reading skill (Winn 1985, 85). Preschool teachers, too, see a change in the general behavior of children since TV has become pervasive, such as increased aggressiveness and decreased verbal skills and independent creativity (113). Naturally, lower verbal skills affect writing skills, and studies have shown students to be decreasingly capable of writing and recognizing coherent and complete thoughts (89).

Winn (1985) recommends that, in addition to parents' controlling their children's TV watching intelligently, students need to study TV in school, to become critical viewers. I wholeheartedly agree, and discuss this and the developmental issues in some detail in the last chapter.

Neil Postman, in his 1985 critique of TV, *Amusing Ourselves to Death*, agrees, saying that TV will be less harmful, if not harmless, if people understand it; the problem is not so much *that* people watch TV as *how* they watch it. "To ask is to break the spell." He says that only the schools can provide the needed instruction and discussion about the nature of TV and its effects, though intense public discussion is also needed.

He is pessimistic, though, pointing out that so far public education has consistently failed to take the responsibility to teach about or demystify the dominant media. He adds that Americans have always been ignorant of the nature of technology in general, including its ideological nature. The almost universally held opinion, even among the "experts," is that technology is neutral, but, as Postman (1985) says, "to make the assumption that technology is always a friend to culture is, at this late hour, stupidity, plain and simple" (157). "Each technology has an agenda of its own," is a "metaphor waiting to unfold" (84).

Media consciousness, not better programming, is the answer, according to Postman (1985). In fact, it would be better for society if TV got worse, for it is not the trashy sitcoms that do the most damage, but the so-called educational and news shows. Even critical programs such as "Saturday Night Live" and "Monty Python" are not emancipatory, argues Postman, for they will inevitably be co-opted by the dominant TV code. As for educational programming, Postman says, in agreement with Winn, that a program like "Sesame Street" doesn't make children love school; it makes them love TV.

Also in agreement with Winn, Postman (1985) argues that TV has done tremendous damage to education. He says that the electronic media have created the third great crisis in Western education, the first being the introduction of the alphabet, and the second, the printing press. The main issue in the current American crisis in education is the difference between reading and watching TV. Television has created the assumption that school, along with every other aspect of life, should be entertaining in the way TV is entertaining. Though many educators are convinced that TV is a valuable educational tool, if not the best one, Postman, a longtime education reformer, insists that the evidence points the other way, that TV is vastly inferior to print in cultivating higher-order inferential thinking.

The most dangerous thing about TV, argues Postman (1985), is that it is the "command center of the new epistemology." It is a "meta-medium," that is, it produces both *what* we know and the *way* we know. This new epistemology is invisible—myth, in Roland Barthes's (1972) sense of natural, unconscious, and un-problematic—which means that people hardly raise any questions about it due to their devout belief in technological "progress." TV is our culture—it doesn't even seem bizarre. But Postman warns that this TV culture is very dangerous to the health of individuals and society. Fortunately, there is a growing media literacy movement, and new books, journals, groups, and school programs are appearing, for example, the groundbreaking National Media Literacy Project in New Mexico, which is putting media education in the high schools with plans to include the entire curriculum (McDonald 1993).

People need to learn that TV promotes incoherence and trivi-ality, is hostile to literate ways of knowing, is *only* entertainment, and is transforming our whole culture into a show business spectacle as all society's institutions become subsumed by it. TV has made entertainment the "natural format for the representation of all experience" and "the supra-ideology of all discourse on television" (Postman 1985, 78–80). Like the alphabet and print, the introduction of speed-of-light transmission of images makes cultural revolution without a vote or resistance. It is "ideology without words, and all the more powerful for their absence" (158).

TV is not, of course, the only medium that disseminates in-formation, but it is the *paradigm* for our idea of public informa-tion; it defines the whole information environment as well as our modes of response to it (Postman 1985, 111). For instance, the newspaper *USA Today*, which (partly because of intense adver-tising on TV) has rapidly become the biggest selling daily, has a kind of TV format—short, snappy articles under color pictures. It has also influenced other newspapers, such as *The Christian*

Science Monitor, which switched from its well-known "serious" format to one that is more "user friendly."

Another example is the popular board game Trivial Pursuit, which rewards players for memory of decontextualized fragments of information. It's a game Hirsch's "culturally literate" students would be good at. Postman claims that TV has altered the very meaning of being informed by creating a type of "disinformation"; that is, information that is misleading, misplaced, irrelevant, fragmented, and superficial. This kind of information leads away from knowing, even away from knowing what it means to know. This effect is not, perhaps, deliberate, but is the inevitable result of packaging news as entertainment (107). Media scholar Mark Crispin Miller says that not only is news a product, it plays on our fears and anxieties and, therefore, plays into the hands of the advertisers who offer thirty seconds of relief from the horror of the news (Moyers 1989).

Postman (1985) calls Americans the best entertained and least informed people in the Western world (106). A horrifying thought is that, if people take ignorance to be knowledge, we may have an uncorrectable situation. That the American public seems to be increasingly content to form opinions and make decisions based on wrong or incomplete knowledge bodes ill for efforts to reform their thinking processes and values. Unfortunately, Hirsch's cultural literacy program leads in precisely this direction.

In agreement with Winn, Postman asserts that inestimable damage is done to children by the jarring juxtaposition of unrelated fragments on TV—thirty seconds of bloodbath followed by thirty seconds of Burger King, for example. "Embedded in the surrealistic frame of a television news show is a theory of anti-communication, featuring a type of discourse that abandons logic, reason, sequence, and rules of contradiction" (1985, 105) (appropriate for certain radical art forms, perhaps, but the most common form of such discourse is found in schizophrenia).

In the 1950s the television commercial, now the single most voluminous form of public communication (most forty-year-olds have seen over one million [Postman 1985, 126]), made linguistic discourse obsolete as the basis for product decisions. "By substituting images for claims, the picture commercial made emotional appeal, not tests of truth, the basis of consumer decisions" (127–128). Commercials are dramas—mythologies—about pretty people ecstatically consuming. It is the consumer that is important, not the product. The TV commercial has steered business away from making valuable products to using emotional power to make customers *feel* valuable themselves. That is, "the consumer is a patient assured by psycho-dramas" (127–128). Commercials tell us how to live our lives, and one of the things the philosophy of commercials teaches is that all problems are easily solvable through technology and consuming.

Postman argues that one of the direst effects of TV culture is that the television commercial has become the fundamental metaphor for political discourse. Americans are consumers, not citizens. In other words, TV has devastated political discourse. Image politics alters the meaning of "self-interest." Instead of tangible interests such as union support, our interests now are mostly symbolic and psychological. "Like television commercials, image politics is a form of therapy." As our current leadership confirms, a majority of the American public seem to want their discontents soothed by a candidate with a soothing image rather than our problems solved by a competent person (135). "In the Age of Show Business and image politics, political discourse is emptied not only of ideological content but of historical content as well. . . . We are being rendered unfit to remember" (136–137). It's not even necessary for a president to be lucid anymore; the presidency is a purely visual thing now—a spectacle (Postman in Moyers 1989).

Postman (1985) agrees with Aldous Huxley that "we are in a race between education and disaster." Huxley's warning was that people would be controlled by being made to laugh instead of think, without knowing "what they were laughing about or why they had stopped thinking." Postman believes this dystopic prophecy is in the process of being fulfilled, that we are "amusing ourselves to death" (163).

Another, in some ways even stronger, critical position is taken by an advertising executive turned social activist, Jerry Mander, in his book *Four Arguments for the Elimination of Television* (1978), in which he argues relentlessly that TV is an unreformable threat to sanity and freedom. He argues that there is repressive capitalist ideology not only in the programming of TV, but in the very technology itself. By its very nature, TV can communicate only certain values and not others. In other words, no matter what the content or intended purpose of the program, only the artificial, fragmented, and nonhuman is actually conveyed. The complexity of human lives and issues is reduced to the proportions of a product being sold in a commercial. The medium is prefectly suited for *selling,* and nothing more.

Mander claims that whoever controls the process of recreation effectively redefines reality for everyone else. He extrapolates from this that whoever controls TV controls society. He thinks that we are not very far away from an efficient totalitarian state in which an all-powerful executive of political bosses and their army of managers control a population of slaves who do not have to be coerced because they love their slavery. This scenario is well depicted in George Orwell's *Nineteen Eighty-Four* (1949). Such leadership would emerge organically at the moment when human experience had been sufficiently channeled and confined. In an atmosphere of mass sensory deprivation, simple, clear statements assume greater authority and profundity than they deserve. Whoever recognizes that such a crucial moment has arrived, that people's minds are sufficiently confused and receptive, can speak directly into them without interference. The people are preconditioned to accept what they hear. This sounds very much like what Reis and Trout say about how effective advertising works.

Judging from today's political climate, the moment may have arrived. We are talking about a subtle coup with no military intervention necessary. Mander is not the first social scientist to espouse such a theory. There is dramatic evidence to support his argument in the constant, usually successful efforts of owners and investors to ensure that there is ideologically pure programming in the media. Making a comparison with *Nineteen Eighty-Four,* Mander suggests that there are millions of American families who would not take a permanently lit TV screen to be a hardship. "In Oceania, Big Brother won't let you turn the set off. In America, little brother" (Mander 1978, 67–69). Dramatic evidence of this was seen during the Gulf War, when the American public was glued to their TVs, watching endless repetition of the same few deceptive bits of war coverage, resulting in their overwhelming support for a war they understood practically nothing about.

We do not need Mander to tell us that Big Business is in control of TV—a few corporations, a few individuals. As luck (and planning) would have it, what can be conveyed best through the medium of TV are the ways of thinking and the kinds of information that best suit the people in control—themes of hate, fear, jealousy, winning, wanting, and violence—the stuff free enterprise is made of. Advertising always reflects the facts and opinions of the people paying for it; therefore, if you accept the existence of advertising, you accept a system designed to persuade and dominate minds by interfering in people's thinking patterns and affecting social evolution.

Ben Bagdikian points out that advertisers often specify content that they do and do not want, and above all they do not want any criticism of the system of contemporary enterprise. For example, Procter & Gamble, TV's biggest advertiser, has established explicit directives for programs it sponsors: "Where it seems fitting, the characters in Procter & Gamble dramas should reflect recognition and acceptance of the world situation in their thoughts and actions, although in dealing with war, our writers should minimize the 'horror' aspects. . . . There will be no material on any of our programs which could in any way further the concept of business as cold, ruthless, and lacking all sentiment or spiritual motivation. . . . Ministers, priests, and similar representatives of positive social forces shall not be cast a villains," and so on (Bagdikian 1983, 158–159).

Mander shares Yankelovitch's concern that people are confused by what the freedom of democracy means, that they confuse the freedom of choice of consumer goods with the freedom of choice of lifestyles. "If I choose a Ford and you choose a Volvo, this is not diversity but unity: consuming" (Mander 1978, 130). TV promotes the tendency of capitalist society to redesign people to live life as a representation of itself (130). A humanlike environment is redesigned into a format that fits a commercial format. Oceania's telescreens provide only an illusion of public life. In putting private life to an end, the telescreen transmissions also put an end to the way people get at the truth. They intensify disconnectedness at the very moment that they create the illusion of community.

People are not paying attention to nature and themselves. They have been deluded into thinking that science and technology can solve all problems. TV reduces our sensitivity to nature, and moving away from knowledge about natural sources produces technocrats, reasons Mander. TV claims to convey nature, the arts, the news, and the details of human feeling. Humans who view these attempts are led to believe that these "fuzzy little pellets of information" about our rich, subtle, complex, and varied world constitute something close to reality. But what they actually do is make the world as fuzzy, coarse, and turned off as the medium itself (Mander 1978, 282).

Interestingly, high resolution TV is creating hard bright pellets—like Christmas candy. A different metaphor suggesting a more seductive hyperreality to project into the world. I think I am seeing life imitate TV when I see young women with big bright blonde hair, pink cheeks, red lips, and blue eyelids—that eerie soap-opera replicant look which I fear is considered by some to be a vision of perfection to measure themselves up against and aspire to. Others, of course, prefer the MTV look, wearing skimpy, skin-tight black things. As passive observers and consumers of spectacle, people, especially young people, are constructing their images in the image of celebrities, and losing themselves in the process (Moyers 1989). (See Appendix for discussion of E. Ann Kaplan's *Rocking Around the Clock: Music Television, Postmodernism and Consumer Culture*.)

The market has become the heart of the visual experience, advertising has appropriated the image, and the validity of an image is dependent upon its ability to be turned into merchandise, says media expert Stuart Ewing (Moyers 1989). We construct, market, and narcissistically consume our own image and that of others; therefore, everyone becomes merchandise. The disco has become the temple of this "meatmarket" mentality. Multimedia marketing extravaganzas create a unidimensionality of imagery—packaged ideas and images that seal off a larger sensibility and compress the imagination. Someone else is always creating our fantasies for us (Moyers 1989).

Mander's conclusion is that TV cannot convey life. Life is not

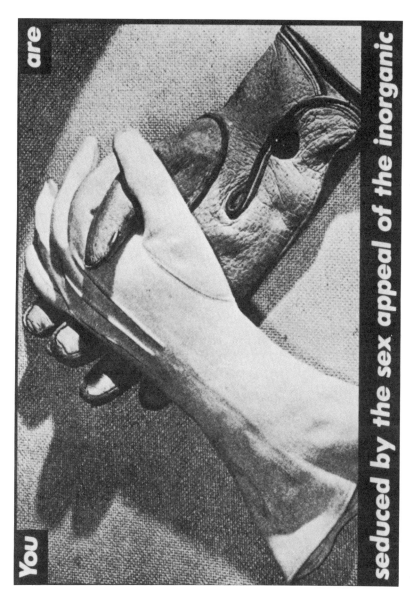

You are seduced by the sex appeal of the inorganic

Photograph by Barbara Kruger, 1982. Used by permission.

lived in separate and distinct boxes. But we can imagine we are not connected to things when our connections are blocked, altered, or stunted. TV stunts the creativity required for making connections—the most crucial activity in human cognitive development, as I will show later.

As we continue to separate ourselves from direct experience of the planet, the hierarchy of technoscientism advances. Mander quotes Michael Bakunin: "The reign of scientific intelligence [will be] the most aristocratic, arrogant, and elitist of all regimes. There will be a new class, a new hierarchy of real and counterfeit scientists and scholars, and the world will be divided into a minority ruling in the name of knowledge, and an immense ignorant majority. And then, woe unto the mass of ignorant ones" (cited in Mander 1978, 61).

Mander cites R. D. Laing's contention that the growing incidence of mental illness these days may be explained in part by the fact that the world we call real and ask people to live within and understand is itself open to question. Mander claims that the major source of this confusion about what is real is TV. Without concrete reality or contact with planetary roots, people are adrift in their own minds; all information has become believable and not believable at the same time. Americans have become the first people in history to live predominantly inside projections of their own minds.

Humans are veritable image factories. When people lose control of their images, then they have lost control of their minds (Mander 1978, 260). The images on TV do not exist in the world. The retina collects impressions emanating from dots and the picture is formed only after it is well inside the brain. The images pass through the eyes in a dematerialized form—invisible. They are reconstituted only after they are already inside the head. This quality of nonexistence, at least in concrete worldly form, may, research already suggests, interfere with conscious thinking. TV qualifies as a kind of wakeful dreaming, except that it is someone else's dream. If TV images have any similarity to dream imagery, this would help explain a growing confusion between the concrete and the imaginary. TV is becoming real to many people, while their own lives take on the quality of a dream.

With terrifying irony, TV defines itself to us as that which gives us, benignly and for free, an ever more and more direct experience of reality, of the whole world, and beyond. And many, maybe most, of us believe it! But the more we believe it, the less true it is.

A big problem is that humans have not been equipped by evolution to distinguish in our minds between natural images and those that are artificially created and implanted (Mander 1978, 216). This fact and the human bias toward belief, which I will discuss later, are what allows TV its exploitative potential, Mander claims. Mechanical reproduction of images is the great equalizer. By the simple process of removing images from immediate experience and passing them through a machine, humans lose one of the attributes that differentiate us from objects. Products suffer no loss, therefore making them more "real" than us. We need theories of the image, which will be an essential part of teaching critical cognitive activity. Such theories are now being developed in recognition of the dominance of the image in mass media today and in popular culture in general.

Mander contributes to Winn's argument when he shows that the technology of TV and the inherent nature of viewing experience actually inhibit learning as we usually think of it, allowing very little cognitive recallable, analyzable, thought-based learning. The evidence is that not only does TV destroy the capacity of the viewer to attend, it also, by taking over a complex of direct and indirect neural pathways, decreases vigilance—the general state of arousal that prepares the organism for action should its attention be drawn to a specific stimulus (Mander 1978, 205). The individual, therefore, may be looking at the unexpected or interesting, but cannot act upon it in such a way as to complete the purposeful processing gestalt. Trancelike fixation is not attention but distraction, which inhibits neural pathways. An external sign that active thinking is not going on is that the eyes are fixed when watching TV. The viewer is in a passive, but also frustrated, state (202).

To really learn anything, you have to interact with the source of the data; you do not interact with TV, though TV itself constantly persuades you to believe that you do, thus concealing the motives and powers that drive it. If our minds are strained, it is from confinement within one pattern of thought. Most of our

mental capacities have gone soft, have atrophied due to underwork (Mander 1978, 212), just as our physical capacities have
gone soft due to underwork. There are already studies that verify
the hypothesis that people remember less that they "learn" from
TV than what they "learn" from print. One particular study
made in February 1991 suggested that the more people watched
news of the Gulf War on TV, the more ignorant they were of the
facts (Cockburn 1991, 330).

Mander is a kind of new Marshall McLuhan, but his message,
unlike McLuhan's, cannot be co-opted by the very technology
he analyzes, because he has only one unequivocal point to
make—eliminate TV. He learned from McLuhan and evaluated
his ideas in the light of the almost twenty years since McLuhan
wrote his major works. Whereas McLuhan had a belief in an
almost mystical reversal of the principles he persuades us to acknowledge, Mander goes to the other extreme in categorically
and cynically denouncing the one technology he is concerned
with. His ideas are so out of step with mainstream thinking that
he has probably been largely ignored or dismissed as a hope-
lessly eccentric crank, but Mander's arguments are very important and all his points should be taken very seriously and
studied further.

However, regardless of their validity, television is not going
to go away any time soon. But the fact that TV is here to stay
does not render Mander's position irrelevant by any means. On
the contrary, the more we face up to the horrors that plague us,
the better we can, if not eliminate them, cope with them. And,
as Postman says, the best way may be to understand them,
though as image theorist Mark Crispin Miller points out, it is
not enough to simply be aware that one is being manipulated.
People must learn to understand the mechanisms of doublethink:
the ability to accept contradiction allows one to be persuaded by
the media images while knowing what is happening (Moyers
1989). To get beyond this requires a concerted effort like learning
to read—indeed, one is learning to read images critically. All
images and montages of images have a built-in strategy of per-
suasion that we must learn to read. Our best teachers may be
the filmmaker theorists such as Eisenstein and Tarkovsky. We
have to learn to make connections between seemingly unrelated

images and events—to see, for example, the waste and destruction of the environment which is silent beneath the image where so many social problems hide from the amused, dazed and confused postliterate eye. Bill Moyers says that images are the basis of our daily decisions, and if we do not as a society become critical viewers, "we'll have no life left but consuming images," for never before have so many images been produced and reached so deep into our consciousness. "At stake is our sense of truth and beauty" (Moyers 1989).

McLuhan seemed to view TV and electronic communication as the Second Coming, a phoenix rising from the ashes of print and alphabetic writing. Walter Ong calls it "secondary orality" (Ong 1982). Both see it as a kind of evolved return to tribal nonliteracy. But rather than seeing it as the best of both worlds, the tribal and the literate, it may be the worst—mechanical orality. Neither McLuhan nor Ong are political enough to worry about who is running the "tribe." Whatever one may think, though, of McLuhan's "global village" resonating in universal harmony, he has invaluable insights into and knowledge of technology, society, and communication that are relevant to this investigation.

McLuhan is famous for this statement: "The medium is the message." This is the cryptic thesis of one of McLuhan's seminal works, *Understanding Media* (1964), taken up on the last two decades by French avante-garde critical theorist Jean Baudrillard. The basic point is that there is important meaning in the physical form one uses as a vehicle for communication, important meaning that may in some ways overshadow the meaning of the particular thoughts that constitute the message; moreover, the message is inextricable from the medium, since they evolved through cultural history together, and thus share common origins.

In two of his major works, *The Gutenberg Galaxy* (1962) and *Understanding Media* (1964), McLuhan expounds his interpretation of the history and meaning of communication technology. Much of *The Gutenberg Galaxy* is scholarly to the point of pedantic as he documents the effects of print on mankind, and much of *Understanding Media* is cryptic to the point of mystical as McLuhan "becomes" the "global village."

McLuhan says *Understanding Media* is concerned with "all

forms of transport of goods and information, both as metaphor and as exchange. Each form of transport not only carries, but translates and transforms, the sender, the receiver, and the message. The use of any kind of medium or extension of man alters the patterns of interdependence among people, as it alters the ratios among our senses. . . . [A]ll technologies are extensions of our physical and nervous systems to increase power and speed" (1964, 91). All media transform experience into new forms beginning with spoken language, which allows people to deal with the environment differently (64). But it is the phonetic alphabet that is the basis of civilization, argues McLuhan, the main features of which are uniform codes, space and time continuity, and individuality. Phonetic literacy translates the "resonating tribal world into Euclidean lineality and visuality" (28). "By the meaningless sign linked to the meaningless sound we have built the shape and meaning of Western man" (1962, 65).

It is one of McLuhan's central claims that nonliterate people identify themselves with the world much more than literate people; that is, the separation and concentration of one of the senses, the visual sense, from the others, detaches people from their holistic involvement with their environment. People in literate society are no longer as sensitive to the radical heterogeneity of reality. The linear movement of literary narrative awareness is foreign to the nature of language and consciousness (McLuhan 1962, 191). The printed word exists because of the technological potential for a fixed point of view, for separating, compartmentalizing, and specializing (155). The printing press expanded this connection of knowledge and sight, providing the "first uniformly repeatable commodity, the first assembly-line, and the first mass production" (153). Print is a consumer medium and commodity; it taught people how to organize all their activities on a systematic lineal basis, how to create markets and national armies.

For McLuhan, it is essential to understand the nature of technology, in general, in order to understand the technology of communication. Technology, he says, is oexplicitness. Concerned with one sense only, technology is the mechanical principle of abstraction and repetition. To make use of any technology is to accept it and to undergo the displacement of perception that automatically follows (1964, 55). He says there is a relationship among the senses, which he calls a "ratio," that is disturbed by technology, which is, by definition, mechanical externalization of a bodily function outside the body—vehicles are extensions of walking, writing of speaking, and so on. McLuhan argues that this artificial limb, as it were, operating outside the body and somewhat beyond the individual's control (à la Frankenstein's creature), has a "numbing" effect on the natural human function, thus making the production of technology something of an "amputation" of human parts. Technology, then, shifts the balance among the senses. A very important point of McLuhan's that very few people seem to take seriously is that it is impossible to construct a theory of cultural change unless one knows about the changing sense ratios effected by various externalizations of our senses (1962, 56).

According to McLuhan, William Blake was also concerned with the notion that when sense ratios change, people change. Blake, in "Jerusalem," wrote, "The Spectre is the Reasoning Power in Man, and when separated / From Imagination, and closing itself as in steel in a Ratio / of the Things of Memory, It thence frames Laws and Moralities / To destroy Imagination, the Divine Body, by Martyrdoms and Wars." McLuhan states:

> Imagination is that ratio among the perceptions and faculties which exists when they are not embedded or outered in material technologies. When so outered, each sense and faculty becomes a closed system. Prior to such outering there is entire interplay among experiences. . . . When the perverse ingenuity of man has outered some part of his being in material technology, his entire sense ratio is altered. He is then compelled to behold this fragment of himself "closing itself as in steel." In beholding this new thing, man is compelled to become it. Such was the origin of lineal, fragmented analysis with its remorseless power of homogenization. (McLuhan 1962, 314–315)

As McLuhan put it, "truth is a ratio between the mind and things, a ratio made by the shaping imagination," which is somehow deadened by the intrusion of the mechanical (1962, 318). The problem with technological tools is that they are closed systems. But our private senses are not; they are open systems "endlessly translated into each other in that experience which we call con-sciousness" (1962, 14).

Separating the visual faculty from interaction with the other senses has resulted in most of our experience being left out of consciousness. The unconscious, ever enlarging, is what used to be the tribal nonliterate world (McLuhan 1962, 304). McLuhan suggests that the age of print introduced the first age of the unconscious, since print allowed only a narrow segment of sense to dominate the other senses: "The unconscious is a direct creation of print technology, the ever-mounting slag-heap of rejected awareness" (1962, 292, 293). Well, that is a startling idea, and I don't know exactly what it means, but it I believe it is an insight to be taken seriously and investigated. At the very least, we must accept the proposition that technology has deeply affected our minds and the way we think. Many people don't accept it, and I would like to offer a persuasive argument to them. We serve technologies as if they were minor gods or even religions. We are "servomechanisms" (McLuhan 1964, 55). Electronic technology has created an extension of the central nervous system outside the body. To the extent that this is true, it is "a development that suggests a desperate and suicidal autoamputation" (53). "Electromagnetic technology requires utter human docility and quiescence of meditation such as befits an organism that now wears its brain outside its skull and its nerves outside its hide. . . . Previous technologies were partial and fragmentary, and the electric is total and inclusive" (64). Narcissus may be a good symbol for technology. He became the "servomechanism" of his own image (53). Since we are in the age of the image, the choice seems particularly apt. However, in electronic media, the image is not even one's own—unless one becomes the image in the process of constructing a self.

McLuhan warns that when we allow our senses and nervous systems to be manipulated, we give up our rights. This somnambulist conforming to the new form or structure makes those most deeply immersed in a revolutionary change the least aware of what is going on (McLuhan 1962, 322–323). That is, we can't see the forest for the virtual-reality trees; we can't see the little black box for the endless barrage of bright images.

McLuhan suggests that up until now cultures have been fated

to "the automatic interiorization of their own technologies" (1962, 95). But it should be possible to free ourselves from these subliminal effects. It should be the main purpose of education to help us do so, because it is absurd not to examine the ways technology is determining our lives (1962, 294, 295). McLuhan isn't very optimistic, having never heard of any culture doing what he suggests, but today, at the beginning of 1994, there actually are some countries that are beginning to control the amount and kind of American media events entering their cultures; even in the United States there is a timid beginning of self-monitoring, but no widespread questioning yet, as far as I can see, of media technologies themselves.

McLuhan says that our conventional response to all media, that it is how they are used that counts, is the "numb stance of the technological idiot" (1964, 32). Moreover, with electronic technology, we have a new problem, for print culture gives people a way of thinking that does not prepare them for living in the electronic age (1962, 42). With electronic media, we no longer live "under the spell of the isolated visual sense. We have not yet begun to ask under what new spell we exist" (1962, 220).

McLuhan is very negative in his assessment of some of the effects of literacy on society, pointing over and over to the dehumanization, homogenization, fragmentation, and mechanization of Western people who are completely oblivious to the forces that shape them: "How is one to reason with the person who feeds himself into a buzz-saw because the teeth are invisible?" He has also been very hard on the education establishment, calling it, among other things, "the homogenizing hopper into which we toss our integral tots for processing" (1962, 257). Yet McLuhan holds out the hope that, somehow, electronic technology will bring everything full circle, back to a kind of enlightened tribal mentality with which all humanity can return to full, balanced use of all senses for a sane, cooperative life in harmony with nature. His friend and colleague Walter Ong also speaks of a "new age of secondary orality" (Ong 1982). But I think a more realistic, though less optimistic, interpretation of the theories, data, and opinions I have presented so far is that we cannot abandon literacy, whatever its legacy. If I understand McLuhan correctly, I worry about his optimism. The *electronic* global village is an illusion. It is a dangerously misleading image, I think: The electronic global network is the *antithesis* of a village. That should be obvious to anyone who has watched international CNN critically for a day or so.

Electronic media is perhaps the ultimate extension of the principles of literacy set in motion thousands of years ago. I doubt that it represents salvation from the hold literacy has on society and our individual minds, but rather I think it represents the full realization of the same drive for power and control that has always driven technology. We must look elsewhere not for a replacement of literacy, but for a way to set ourselves free from its shackles, a way to go beyond literacy.

According to French sociologist/philosopher Jean Baudrillard, McLuhan's Nietzschean successor, all is lost—media domination is complete—the subject is dead, and there is no more possibility of meaning. Over and over he argues "THE MEDIUM IS THE MESSAGE" (Baudrillard 1973, 35). He says the implications of this statement are far from being exhausted. "The medium is the message" is the "key formula of the era of simulation." It is the medium that controls the process of meaning. "All the contents of meaning are absorbed in the dominant form of the medium. The medium alone makes the event" (100–101).

However, carrying McLuhan to an even more extreme conclusion, Baudrillard claims that "there is not only the implosion of the message in the medium; in the same movement there is the implosion of the medium itself in the real, *the implosion of the medium and the real* in a sort of nebulous hyperreality where even the definition and the distinct action of the medium are no longer distinguishable" (1973, 100). In other words, "The medium is the message" signifies not only the end of the message, but also the end of the medium, that is, there is no longer "a power mediating between one reality and another, between one state of the real and another—neither in content nor in form." This is what "implosion" means: "the absorption of one pole into another, the short-circuit between poles of every differential system of meaning, the effacement of terms and of distinct oppositions, and thus that of the medium and the real" (1973, 102).

Baudrillard is arguing that we are no longer "subjects," actors in our own private dramas in time and space, but have been reduced to McLuhan's condition of complete "autoamputation," complete exteriorization of the human senses, "electronic 'encephalization' and miniaturization of circuits and energy, transistorization of the environment," which "relegates to total uselessness . . . all that used to fill the scene of our lives." That is, TV has made reality archaic, perplexing and useless, because human action has been "crystallized" on screens and terminals. The TV is the "ultimate and perfect object" for this era; "our own body and the whole surrounding universe become a control screen." Baudrillard maintains, "The most intimate processes of our life become the virtual feeding ground of the media" when "all becomes transparence and immediate visibility, when everything is exposed to the harsh and inexorable light of information and communication" (Baudrillard 1983a, 127–130). We see this every day on the increasing number of daytime talk shows, which dig and pry deeper into the intimate details of people's lives. Rapists, wife beaters, murderers, child molestors, adulterers, prostitutes, multiple personality patients, and pregnant teenagers appear on TV to tell their stories to often unsympathetic audiences.

Baudrillard would seem to agree with Postman that self-expression and meaning have been appropriated by mass media culture, leaving the masses with nothing but "spectacle"—useless, amusing distractions. Baudrillard argues that, counterintuitively, information destroys or neutralizes meaning. It is a myth, he says, that information produces meaning and socialization. The opposite is true: "information devours its own content; it devours communication and the social." Information "exhausts itself in the staging of meaning . . . a gigantic process of simulation. . . . Behind this exacerbated staging of communication, the mass media, with its pressure of information, carries out an irresistible destructuration of the social" (1973, 96–100). This makes Hirsch's cultural literacy even more insidious. His "information" will block students from developing into communicating, social beings.

Here is a crucial point: all media and all information act in two directions at once; outwardly they produce more of the social, and inwardly they neutralize social relations and the social itself. The appearance of the social conceals that it is only "*an effect* of the social, a simulation and an illusion" (1973, 66). The masses absorb all the social energy, all messages, but never respond, reflect, or participate. Mander agrees. I agree. I will show in chapter 5 that this is indeed the opposite of the conditions set forth by Vygotsky for the development of individuals and society—goal-oriented participation in the activities of society and personal life.

The age of simulation is characterized by "a liquidation of all referentials"; there are no more referents, no more representation—all signification refers to that which is not real but only simulacra of the real (Baudrillard 1983b, 4). Therefore, for Baudrillard there seems to be no possibility anymore for critical distance. Criticism is reduced to a "grotesque simulacrum of what it used to be," and "all that remains is the fascination for arid and indifferent forms, for the very operation of the system which annuls us" (Foss 1984, 9). Perhaps he exaggerates. I believe that meaningful criticism is still possible—maybe more powerful than ever—but I don't think Baudrillard wants us to take all his theatrics literally; we don't have to, in any case.

This desperate and hopeless situation must be acknowledged, insists Baudrillard. He says that the only hope we have is to think this situation through to the end. "It is the only one we are left with. It is useless to dream of a revolution through content or through form, since the medium and the real are now in a single nebulous state whose truth is undecipherable. . . . The fact of this implosion of contents, of absorption of meaning, . . . of the implosion of the social in the masses, can appear catastrophic and hopeless. But it is so only in regard to the idealism that dominates our whole vision of information" (Baudrillard 1973, 103). There may be some hope, but all we can do, says Baudrillard, is push the system to its limits, breach the code with symbolic disorder, take the play of simulation further than the system permits, and hope for some sort of reversal (Kellner 1989, 127–128)—hence postmodernism. Though this cryptic notion echoes McLuhan, Baudrillard does not seem to have McLuhan's happy vision of the global village, but some dark unknowable new stage of civilization. I agree with Baudrillard.

In his critique of Baudrillard, Douglas Kellner argues that Baudrillard is overstating the case against media; he claims that the media do not prevent emancipatory or subversive communication, that they are contested terrain, "an arena of struggle in which social conflicts are articulated and worked out" (1989, 136–137). For Kellner, the value of Baudrillard is to shock us into an awareness that "we are living in a transitional situation where new social conditions are putting into question the old orthodoxies and boundaries." Baudrillard may force us to "put into question conventional disciplinary wisdom and rethink contemporary radical social theory and politics in the light of changing sociohistorical conditions. . . . We may be living on the frontier between the modern and the post-modern and could be entering a phase in which old modes of thought and language are not of much help" (143–144). Precisely.

Martin Heidegger, in his essay "The Question Concerning Technology" (1977), says that there is a danger of people being so caught up in the technological mentality that they do not realize that they are missing any dimensions of reality. To the extent that Baudrillard is right, Heidegger's worst fears have been realized. Modern society, personal life, and culture in general, are indeed suffocating from obsession with the technological mode of thinking while, ironically, believing themselves to be liberated by it.

In response to these changes, the concept of a postmodern world has been evolving over the past several years. There is heated debate over what this term might mean, but in general it is an idea that society and culture and the ways people interact with reality have changed in some fundamental ways. Baudrillard's critique may be considered postmodern. There are many differing theories of postmodernity as well as theories, practices, and commentaries on postmodern artistic expressions. There are negative condemnations of a sensibility based on impotent resignation to the way things are, a sensibility that makes the situation worse by choosing to wallow in decadence rather than attempting to contribute to constructive change. But there are also those, including myself, who see the concept of postmodernism as useful in defining and analyzing new aspects of today's art and culture.

An example of the testy and defensive, even hateful, anti-intellectualism that characterizes much of the American "intellectual'' community is a review by Daniel Harris in the June 1990 Boston Phoenix Literary Section of Baudrillard's *Seduction.* So typical of reactionaries, Harris lambasts the American academic community in general for its "blind servility" to the "lunatic fringe of intellectually marginal groups"—followers of Derrida, Lacan, Baudrillard, and the like—and "making a religion out of the state of confusion," when, in fact, as far as I can tell, most of the American academic community basically agrees with him! He says it is only fear and insecurity that make people pretend to get some meaning from texts such as *Seduction* (or anything by Baudrillard): "This illicit thrill and false bravado, the insinuation that they are all members of an elite group of the initiated, provides a soothing anodyne for the bruised academic ego that is increasingly anxious about its own cultural irrelevance. The arcane self-involvement of the contemporary theorist is nothing more than the internalization of our culture's contempt and indifference—a pervasive malaise into which academics have burrowed like hamsters to lick their wounds with riddles and cryptgrams.''

Now, how can we hope to solve difficult problems that require new ways of thinking, new theories, new ideas, new strategies if we have this kind of knee-jerk negative reaction to everything new, difficult, or strange, even ideas taken very seriously by many reputable scholars and intellectuals all over the world? Arrogance like Harris's is the real villain, of course—not the texts of French thinkers or Americans who are open-minded and energetic enough to explore and discuss them.

Harris displays one of the nastiest traits of the American ethos in and out of academe, believing that anything one does not understand or appreciate must, therefore, be worthless, even immoral. I do not think everyone or anyone should feel obliged to read everything or anything by everyone or anyone in the French poststructuralist school (if one may create such a category), any more than I think everyone or anyone ought to study quantum physics. But to ridicule or make any comment whatsoever about texts that one has not been trained to read is truly asinine. Harris is like a fanatical creationist; he is judging something he knows nothing about.

In his "review" (which is actually a refusal to review), he says he doesn't describe the content of this work of Baudrillard that he is supposed to be reviewing because "it has no content other than his empty, obfuscating gestures and his naked impulse to domineer and frustrate." This could all be forgotten—thrown into the dustbin of bad journalism—if it weren't for the fact that it is symptomatic of a great cultural ill, the refusal to bend from old traditional thinking and to consider new ideas. Harris probably can't do much harm besides throwing fuel on the verbal book-burning fire, but the many academics who think as he does are doing tremendous harm to students by nipping in the bud what little curiosity some few of them may have about what is happening on the cutting edge of critical cultural theory.

There are, however, many important and insightful essays and works of art that affirm the notion of postmodernism and instruct us about the new and confusing aspects of contemporary culture. I won't get into a lengthy discussion of postmodernism here, but will briefly mention two American critics who have interesting ideas on the subject: Susan Suleiman and Todd Gitlin. Gitlin says that postmodernism, which is specifically though not exclusively American, is characterized by textuality instead of unity; it is "a cultivation of surfaces endlessly referring to, ricocheting from, reverberating onto other surfaces" (Gitlin 1989, 102). "Anything can be juxtaposed to anything else." It is "cultural recombination" (105). It is an attempt to find a language for articulating new understanding about today's world. It is political in the sense that it wants to reveal and critique the dominant culture and the power it has over us. Though some postmodern expressions may only be mimicking the chaotic inanity of our culture, others may be a challenge to that culture, using it against itself by making us look at it in a new way and therefore think about it.

Suleiman says that postmodernism may be mostly the way a text is read rather than anything inherent in the text; in other words, regardless of the intent behind a work of art or any text, a postmodern sensibility can read analysis and critique of culture into it. She defines a postmodern style as "the appropriation, misappropriation, montage, collage, hybridization, and general mixing up of visual and verbal texts and discourses, from all periods of the past as well as from the multiple social and linguistic fields of the present" (Suleiman 1990, 191–193). She cites Linda Hutcheon, who calls postmodern work ambivalent and contradictory, a doubly encoded "challenge to culture from within," and Craig Owens, who calls postmodernism the "true art of deconstruction, for it recognizes the unavoidable necessity of participating in the very activity that is being denounced precisely in order to denounce it" (Suleiman 1990, 196).

I believe that a postmodern sensibility is necessarily implied in the new paradigm for education that will address the realities of today's world, and in the appendix I will discuss some examples of postmodern texts and readings that can be used in the classroom for teaching critical cognitive activity.

This chapter has presented contemporary culture as rife with complex and, to some extent, new problems that are imperfectly understood. What follows is a discussion of breakthroughs and new paradigms in a variety of disciplines which can be connected to formulate a new paradigm for education, and, by extension, society. Our society can form a new basis for coping with the problems outlined in this chapter, a new framework for making the best use of the old and new knowledge and ways of thinking that are available to us in teaching critical cognitive activity to students, whose development has been arrested by their own culture.

> They say that heaven is like TV—a perfect little world that
> doesn't really need you—and everything there is made of
> light—and the days keep going by—here they come.
> —*Laurie Anderson**

*From "Strange Angels" by Laurie Anderson. © 1989 Difficult Music.

III

In Search of New Paradigms

"Let X equal X."

—*Laurie Anderson**

Many thinkers in many different disciplines and fields of study are seeing the need for a new paradigm within which to work, having reached a dead end working within their old ones, which have been based on the Newtonian mechanistic paradigm. In order to solve the problems I have outlined so far, I believe a new paradigm is necessary. Indeed, I believe that many of the problems have been caused by the inadequacies and misapplications of the old paradigm.

In this chapter, I will attempt to show new scientific paradigms and discoveries that have informed my search for increased understanding of and strategies for solving the interconnected problems of contemporary American society and education. Since the problems seem to elude the strategies generated by the traditional Newtonian mechanistic paradigm, it is necessary to look for a new one. From my ongoing investigation of several scientific disciplines, I have concluded that the basis

*From "Let X = X" by Laurie Anderson. © 1984 Difficult Music.

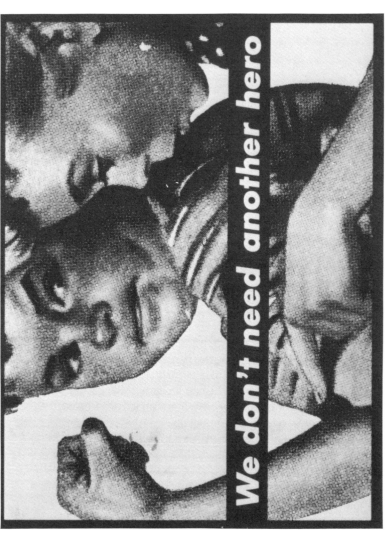

We don't need another hero

Photograph by Barbara Kruger, 1986. Used by permission.

for a new paradigm for education and society already exists and is gaining momentum among cutting-edge thinkers all across the disciplines and the academic curriculum. It is this new, emerging paradigm that I will try to characterize, in addition to presenting recent discoveries and theories about the way humans think, solve problems, and form and change worldviews and belief systems. It is these ideas and those in the next two chapters that I find relevant to the project of learning the kinds of thinking and teaching that should form the basis of a new paradigm for education and critical cognitive activity.

One discipline that provides new, enabling structures of thought and perceptions about reality is quantum physics. Many progressive thinkers today, philosophic physicists and nonphysicists with various specialties, are talking about the possible applications of certain aspects of quantum physics to philosophical problems. Although the more traditional members of the physics community debunk these efforts, they serve some people as ways of prodding the creative thought processes and providing a structure of useful metaphors for perceiving reality differently.

For example, Gary Zukov, in his book on philosophy and quantum physics *The Dancing Wu Li Masters*, says that quantum logic is not only more exciting than classical logic, it is more "real," that is, it is not based upon the restricted and distorted way that classical logic has us think of things, but more nearly upon the way we experience them. The wave-particle duality has freed physics for radical new ways of perceiving reality. It marks the end of either/or thinking. In the realm of experience, nothing is either this or that. There is always at least one more alternative and often an unlimited number. But the way we pose our questions often seems to limit our responses to a perspective of either/or, though experience itself is never so limited.

Philosophically, Bohr's principle of complementarity, which explains wave-particle duality; that is, that one can trace subatomic entities as waves or as particles, but not both simultaneously, leads to the conclusion that the world consists not of things but of interactions, that properties belong not to things but to interactions, and that this is true for everything, all phenomena. Moreover, there exists an ambiguity barrier beyond which we can never pass without venturing into the realm of uncertainty. This discovery, known as Heisenberg's uncertainty principle, shows that we cannot observe phenomena without changing it. The physical properties that we observe in the "external world" are enmeshed in our own perceptions, not only psychologically but ontologically as well. Because both particle and wave can be ascribed to light, it appears that light has no properties independent of us. Without us, "light" doesn't exist.

There is a theory in physics, Bell's theorem, which says that at a deep and fundamental level, the "separate parts" of the universe are connected in an intimate and immediate way. If correct, this theorem shows that commonsense ideas are inadequate for describing even macroscopic events of the everyday world. If all the separate parts of the universe are manifestations of the same whole and there is only one unified reality, then physics may require a more complete alteration of our thought processes than we Westerners have ever conceived (Bohm 1980, 256).

Einstein's ultimate vision is that there are no such things as "gravitational fields" and "masses." They are only mental constructs. There is nothing but space-time and motion, and they, in effect, are the same thing. Here is an exquisite presentation in completely Western terms of the most fundamental aspect of Taoism and Buddhist philosophy. Quantum mechanics tells us the same thing that Tantraic Buddhists have been saying for a millenium: the connection between the "dots" is a product of our minds. It is not really "there" (Bohm 1980, 198).

The major contribution of quantum mechanics to Western thought may be its impact on the artificial categories by which we structure our perceptions. Ossified structures of perception are the prisons in which we become unknowing prisoners. According to some Eastern philosophies, opposites are false distinctions, mental structures we have created. These false distinctions are abstractions from experience that we have mistaken for experience. Perhaps we have lived so long in our abstractions that, instead of realizing that they are *drawn* from the real world, we believe that they *are* the real world. Whether or not something is true is not a matter of how closely it corresponds to absolute truth but of how consistent it is with our own experiences. Why, asks Zukov, should we make one particular frame of reference privileged in respect to all others by saying that it, all alone, is absolutely not moving (1979, 135)?

The idea that objects exist apart from events is part of the epistemological net with which we snare our particular form of experience. This idea is dear to us because we have accepted it without question as the basis of our reality. The philosophical implication of quantum mechanics is that all of the things in our universe (including us) that appear to exist independently are actually parts of one all-encompassing organic pattern and that the distinction between organic and inorganic is a conceptual prejudice. John Von Neumann's discovery that our thought processes (the realm of symbols) project illusory restrictions onto the real world is essentially the same discovery that led Einstein to the theory of relativity. His work pointed to a fusion of ontology, epistemology, and psychology. In short, he said the problem is in the language (Zukov 1979, 260).

Symbols do not follow the same rules as experience. They follow rules of their own. A description of a state of being is a symbol. Quantum logic, though itself a symbolic structure, calls us back from the realm of symbols to the realm of experience. The Copenhagen interpretation of quantum mechanics destroys the scientific belief in absolute truth and does away with the idea of a one-to-one correspondence between reality and theory. This suggests that the world is in some way profoundly different from our ordinary ideas about it; therefore, it might not be possible to construct a model of reality, because all the mind can ponder is its *ideas* about reality (Zukov 1979, 38). It appears that there is a recognition emerging throughout the West that knowledge itself is limited. These concepts about reality from quantum physics are the principles deconstruction is built on, as I will show in the next chapter.

According to Chinese particle physics, the world is fundamentally *wu li*, "dancing energy." In this worldview there is no substance; it is a picture of chaos beneath order. Zukov points to the view of quantum physicist–philosopher David Bohm that a new "instrument of thought" is needed, a new instrument of thought that Zukov says would radically alter the consciousness of the observer, reorienting it toward a perception of the "unbroken wholeness of which everything is a form" (1979, 311).

In his book *Wholeness and the Implicate Order,* David Bohm (1980) concedes that it is very difficult not to treat knowledge as a set of basically fixed truths instead of descriptions of moments in a process, moments which are abstractions from the indescribable flux of reality. The form of our language continually introduces a tendency toward fragmentation, thus putting a strong but subtle unconscious pressure on us to hold a fragmentary worldview. As much as possible, Bohm says, our atomistic attitude toward words should be dropped and replaced with a particle physics view that would see words as only "convenient abstractions from the whole movement," and language as "an undivided field of movement" (41).

Bohm's ideas about language are much the same as those of theorists such as L. S. Vygotsky, Kenneth Burke, Roland Barthes, and Jacques Derrida: One must understand that there is a worldview contained in every language and must be able to see when her or his worldview/language fails to correlate well with experience and observation (Bohm 1980, 47). "Thought with totality as its content has to be considered as an art form, like poetry, whose function is primarily to give rise to a perception, and to action implicit in this perception, rather than to communicate reflective knowledge of 'how everything is.' This implies that there can no more be an ultimate form of such thought than there could be an ultimate poem" (63). Of course this is wishful thinking—as far as I know everyone believes that his or her thoughts about reality are precisely the way everything *is!*

Bohm goes on to say that it isn't possible to know where his ideas on thought might lead; we must be open to change as we proceed with the analysis of thought (63). This uncertainty and unpredictability about the future, not only about concrete details of experience but about the order and nature of things, is something Western thinkers have evolved to find abhorrent, unthinkable, and false.

Bohm believes there is an extreme necessity to study thought processes, but notes that there does not seem to be much interest in it, even though the quality of thought is vital to all other studies. He says it is particularly unfortunate that the studies of life and mind are dominated by fragmentary paradigms. If we realized how dangerous such fragmentary thinking is, we would place more importance on studying the thinking process (Bohm 1980, 19). I tried to show in the preceding chapter that the forces at work in the TV culture, including education reformers such as Hirsch, are exacerbating this fragmentation problem, not helping it.

Bohm makes a helpful distinction between "thought" and "intelligence." "Thought," he says, is all basically mechanical, conditioned responses of memory under one word or symbol, whereas "intelligence" is fresh, original, unconditioned perception, "beyond any knowable law," which can see if a particular line of thought is relevant and fitting. Perhaps an intelligent perception is the brain and nervous system responding "directly to an order in the universe and unknown flux that cannot be reduced to anything that could be defined in terms of knowable structures. . . . It is thought, responding to intelligent perception, which is capable of bringing about an overall harmony or fitting between mind and matter" (1980, 53).

But if we don't understand the process of thinking, we will remain conditioned to think that our thoughts are more than thoughts, more than efforts to represent reality, that they actually are reality (Bohm 1980, 62). This misunderstanding prevents the mind from processing experience more openly and creatively. This is where McLuhan and Heidegger say technology leads and where Baudrillard says postmodern society now is (as discussed in chapter 2). We have succumbed to an unrealistic attitude; we are unaware that thought processes do not give a view of the whole of reality.

There is a problem, Bohm says, in the way we learn mechanically to mindlessly accept what we are taught, rather than discovering and appreciating the original insights in what we learn (1980, 24). This is what Socrates said over two millenia ago in the *Phaedrus* and others have said since, which indicts Hirsch's project and modern teaching methods of rote memorization of information, or the mechanical reductions of what were originally creative insights.

Bohm introduces the word *multiplex*, meaning "many complexes all folded together." He uses this word because it better conveys the idea of implicate order than the more common "continuum" (1980, 166). The "law of the whole" requires more than a transcribing of current quantum theory. All of physics must be placed in a new structure in which space, time, matter, and movement are redefined. This will lead to new avenues of thought not possible with current theories (169). What may be needed is a new theory, from which the theory of relativity and quantum theory could be derived as abstractions, approximations, and limiting cases. What relativity and quantum theory have in common is undivided wholeness. Beginning with undivided wholeness requires dropping the mechanistic order (176). Perhaps the new science of chaos is a theory that satisfies Bohm's demands. I will discuss it later in the chapter.

> Though physics has changed radically in many ways, the Cartesian grid ... has remained the one key feature that has not changed. Evidently, it is not easy to change this, because our notions of order are pervasive, for not only do they involve our thinking but also our senses, our feelings, our intuitions, our physical movement, our relationships with other people and with society as a whole and, indeed, every phase of our lives. It is thus difficult to "step back" from our old notions of order sufficiently to be able seriously to consider new notions of order. (Bohm 1980, 176)

Bohm uses the term "implicate order" for basic, primary, independently existent, and universal order. "Explicate order," by contrast, is secondary, derivative, and appropriate in limited contexts. In the prevailing mechanistic approach, the task of science is to start from parts and derive all wholes through abstraction, explaining them as the results of interactions of the parts. Conversely, when one works with the concept of implicate order, one begins with the undivided wholeness of the universe and tries to derive the parts as "approximately separable, stable, and recurrent, but externally related elements making up relatively autonomous sub-totalities, which are to be described in terms of an explicate order" (1980, 178–179). These distinctions and definitions are harmonious with deconstructive thinking, as I will show in the next chapter.

If matter and consciousness can be understood together in the same structure, they can be seen to be related on some common ground (Bohm 1980, 197). "We do not say that mind and body causally affect each other, rather that the movements of both are the outcome of related projections of a common higher dimensional ground" (209).

We no longer, if we ever did, need only the dichotomy of abstract logical thought and concrete immediate experience that is fragmented thinking; we can conceive of flow between the two (Bohm 1980, 203). The implicate order is fundamentally more immediate than the explicate order, which is a construction that has to be learned. But we don't notice the immediacy of implicate order because we emphasize and are used to the constructs of explicate order in our thought and language. Moreover, memory forces us to focus our attention on what is static and fragmented (206). McLuhan has shown how literacy indoctrinates us into these structures.

Bohm himself, acknowledges the great obstacles to his vision, saying that understanding of fragmentation and wholeness requires a level of creativity higher than needed for great achievements in science and art (1980, 24). Yet some of the breakthroughs in science are offering just such new insights.

The new science of chaos is, I think, the perfect model for a new paradigm of reality. James Gleick's book *Chaos: Making a New Science* (1987) provides wonderful stories about the formation of this science that can be applied by anyone who is looking for a new way of thinking. Gleick calls chaos "the paradigm shift of paradigm shifts" (52), the first one for many of the scientists involved, who felt they were seeing a true transformation of thinking following the pattern laid out by Thomas Kuhn: "one account of nature replaces another" (52). Old problems are seen in a new light, and other problems are recognized for the first time. For some, chaos is a science of process rather than static state, a science of becoming rather than being.

Paradigm shifts are rare and difficult to accomplish, according to Thomas Kuhn (1970), because it is inherent in the structure of the modern scientific system that scientists will not be innovators, but problem solvers working within an established system. A paradigm shift—a revolution in science—only occurs when the established tradition has reached a dead end; this is when the most important advances in knowledge are made (Gleick

1987, 36–37). Though Kuhn is speaking about science, I believe the same principles apply to all disciplines and fields of study.

True to Kuhn's described pattern, the evolution of this new science was a rocky road, but now, says Gleick, "chaos seems to be everywhere" (1987, 5). One of the problems in the development of chaos into a legitimate field recognized by the conservative scientific establishment was that it breaks across disciplinary boundaries. Many of the early chaos theorists came from widely diverse fields, such as meteorology, physics, and mathematics. This was a big obstacle to overcome because of the tendency in Western science (and scholarship in general) to keep disciplines separate. But because chaos is a science of the global nature of systems, it has brought together researchers from fields that had been widely separated, making it a model of interdisciplinary and supradisciplinary study, a key feature of the new paradigm that can be seen emerging in many fields today. In fact, chaos may be *the* model for the new paradigm.

For many scientists chaos has brought an end to the reductionist and compartmentalized program in science. But this is happening only after many years—most of the 1970s and 1980s—of hostile resistance. Finally, chaos bore fruit for so many, it couldn't be ignored. Before chaos, nonlinear problems were ignored because no one knew how to approach them, even though to some observers it was clear that chaos was a reality in nature not reflected in the linear model. Now they do know how to approach nonlinear problems. Scientists in many different fields have the need or desire to understand complexity, and chaos is a tool for doing it.

Chaos shot down the following set of shared beliefs: Simple systems behave in simple ways; complex behavior implies complex causes; different systems behave differently. Now the following set of ideas prevails: Simple systems produce complex behavior; complex systems produce simple behavior; the laws of complexity are universal. In fact, the second law of thermodynamics, the universal law of increasing entropy, does not account for the creation of complex order; no such law has been discovered until now, and chaos seems to have uncovered one (Gleick 1987, 303–308).

"Randomness is chaos with feedback," says physicist Joseph

Ford; "The universe is randomness and dissipation, yes. But randomness with direction can produce surprising complexity." Einstein said that god didn't play dice with the universe; Ford says god *does* play dice with the universe, but the dice are loaded. Now physics must learn by what rules they are loaded and how to use those rules (Gleick 1987, 314).

Basically what chaos theory is, is the use of the computer to generate such a heretofore impossibly large number of repetitions of mathematical functions that new aspects of reality are revealed, a new kind of order beneath disorder. Chaos theory opens new doors onto the states of dynamical systems. It is a new key to discovering the nature and significance of scale, randomness, nonlinearity; for example, the interplay of microscale and macroscale that is characteristic of fluid turbulence and other complex dynamical processes (Gleick 1987, 299). In the words of Douglas Hofstadter, "It turns out that an eerie type of chaos can lurk just behind a facade of order—and, yet, deep inside the chaos lurks an even eerier type of order" (cited in Gleick 1987, jacket notes).

The science of chaos has discovered that "life sucks order from a sea of disorder." Or, as Erwin Schrödinger put it forty years ago, before there were the technological tools necessary for analysis beyond a certain point: "A living organism has the 'astonishing gift of concentrating a "stream of order" onto itself and thus escaping the decay into atomic chaos'" (cited in Gleick 1987, 299). Schrödinger intuited what chaos theory now allows to be proven—that aperiodicity, nonlinearity, is not an anomaly, but the *source* of life's special qualities, of creativity. Chaos focuses on the changes in the nature of phenomenological processes at certain points of acceleration or temperature or some other variable, such as the onset of turbulence—the change of a material from one state to another, such as water to vapor. In the new sense, chaos means "orderly disorder created by simple processes." Chaos "pulls the data into visible shapes" (267).

"Sensitive dependence on initial conditions" is a key concept in chaos theory. It refers to the large differences in output that can be effected by very small differences in input; that is, a very small factor can produce very large and significant effects. It is about randomness and complexity, "jagged edges and sudden leaps." A whimsical but partially serious example often given to illustrate this concept is the Butterfly Effect, the idea that a butterfly beating the air with its wings one day in Peking can affect the weather in New York a month later (Gleick 1987, 8). Conventional science has taught that small influences can be neglected, but chaos proves otherwise.

The laboratory of chaos is the computer; computer-generated graphics are the key to chaos research because they create a visual display of millions of moments of movement, all the possibilities in a system over time. They show things that have never been seen before, often counterintuitive things. These displays prove that very small differences in input do, indeed, have great importance—like the straw that broke the camel's back or the hundredth monkey. A system working on itself over and over and over can create unpredictable, bizarre drifts that occur gradually, or even sudden catastrophic reversals.

Another important concept is "phase transitions," the concept that names the phenomenon of matter changing from one state to another, such as water to vapor or laminarity (smooth motion) to turbulence. Like many aspects of chaos, phase transitions are changes of microscopic behavior that seem insignificantly small, but which at some unknowable point become very significant with enormous effects; material becomes a liquid, a magnet, a super-conductor—something it wasn't before (Gleick 1987, 127).

The centerpiece of chaos theory appears to be fractal geometry. Fractal geometry defines shapes, not by solving an equation as in other geometries, but by repeating it in a feedback loop. In this mode the equation becomes a process instead of a description, dynamic instead of static (Gleick 1987, 226–227). An infinitely long line in a finite area is a "fractal." An example is the charting of a geographical coastline. According to Benoit Mandelbrot, a coastline is infinitely long, if one continues to measure all the curves, coves, and bumps closer and closer with a smaller and smaller ruler. Moreover, the degree of irregularity remains constant across scales. "Fractal" means self-similar, symmetry across scales, pattern inside of pattern—a common idea in Western culture, such as the notion of the world in a grain of sand, infinitely regressive reflections in two parallel mirrors, and so on. Things look similar under higher and higher magnification (Gleick 1987, 103).

Fractal geometry allows one to see the organizing structure hidden in complicated shapes. Mandelbrot felt that the simple shapes of Euclidean geometry were inhuman, not natural. "Clouds are not spheres [and] mountains are not cones. Lightning does not travel in a straight line," says Mandelbrot. "The new geometry mirrors a universe that is rough, not rounded, scabrous, not smooth," explains Gleick. "It is a geometry of the pitted, pocked, and broken up, the twisted, tangled, and intertwined." Mandelbrot made a claim about the world: these irregularities have meaning. They are not just distortions of the classic shapes of Euclidean geometry; they signify something about the essence of the world. In other words, Mandelbrot's fractal geometry is "nature's own" (Gleick 1987, 94). Perhaps this is the theory Bohm is looking for to replace a simple linear continuum and one that reinforces deconstructive principles, as I will show in the next chapter.

Chaos presents problems that cannot be solved with the accepted ways of working in science. Gleick says, "Where chaos begins, classical science stops" (3). According to Mandelbrot, understanding the new paradigm involves developing a new intuition. He said he had to train his intuition to accept shapes that he initially rejected as absurd. Fractal geometry produces a new picture of the relationship between order and chaos. Apparently on every scale, however infinitesimally small or large, there exists the similarity of order as well as the difference of chaos—similarity, not identity. As the technologically enhanced computational eye of the scientist moves through a dynamical system from the small scale to the large, it sees order disintegrate into chaos, chaos coalesce toward order, order disintegrate into chaos, and so forth, presumably ad infinitum.

The Mandelbrot Set, an early example of fractal geometry, now famous even among many nonscientists, may be the most complex object in mathematics. Gleick states: "An eternity would not be enough time to see it all," even though the entire set requires only a few dozen characters of code and a simple equation repeated millions of times (221). The Mandelbrot Set produces computer images of graceful swirling shapes made up of smaller-scale versions of similar shapes that are also made up of still smaller-scale similar shapes, ad infinitum. Mandelbrot's intuition was that simplicity breeds complexity, and he proved it by joining the world of shapes to the world of numbers (225). He was looking for a symmetry across every scale, large or small, and found it in the Mandelbrot Set, which contains copies of itself at every level of magnification without any of the parts exactly resembling any other part. One popular use of fractal geometry is in computer simulations of nature. Such natural objects as trees and mountains can be computer generated to look natural; this is called "virtual reality"—the artificial imitation of the irregular but recognizable patterns of nature to create the illusion of photographic reality.

Christopher Scholz, a Columbia University professor specializing in the formation and structure of the solid earth, became a disciple of fractal geometry: He sees it as model that allows us to describe all the changing features of the earth. "Once you . . . understand the paradigm, you can measure and think about things in a new way. You have a new vision." Faults and fractures dominate the structure of the earth's surface and are the key to any good description; they are more important on balance than the material they run through (cited in Gleick 1987, 105–107). In the next chapter, I will try to show that deconstructive thinking is based on the same principles as these concepts of fractal geometry and chaos science, and it is arguable that chaos science is based on deconstructive thinking.

Because the concepts of traditional paradigms, in this case Euclidean geometry, impose a bias on the way one sees, the questions one asks, and so on, it is hard to break away and learn to see in a new way. For example, in biology, the traditional structures and language in anatomical science tend to hide the unity that exists across scales, since anatomists look at only one scale at a time. Now, some theoretical biologists are finding fractal organizations throughout the body. Branching structures, such as a complicated network of fibers in the heart, can now be understood and easily described as fractals with only a few bits of information that specify a repeating process of bifurcation and development. DNA may be the most dramatic instance, with only four differently shaped chemicals constricting billions of pieces of genetic information capable of producing an astonishing variety of complex organisms.

Chaos is the "creation of information"; as a system becomes chaotic it generates "information," that is, something new, unpredictable (Gleick 1987, 260). At the same time, what appears initially to be randomness eventually seems to be drawn toward a point by a force called the "strange attractor." The strange attractor is the hidden force in the dynamic system that is producing significant effects despite the scientists' unawareness of its existence, like a "black star" having a strong gravitational pull on an observed object in space and producing unpredicted movement.

Chaos finds the traces of hidden variables that have influenced the variables being charted. These hidden variables are the strange attractors that eventually, given sufficient repetition, reveal glimmers of pattern and structure peering through masses of chaotic data, like the control genes that switch on the parts of genes needed to produce different parts of a body. The identification of the phenomenon called the strange attractor depends on a powerful invention of chaos science, "phase space." Phase space is a computer-generated picture that is a kind of metaphorical map for all the possible movements of the parts of a dynamical system throughout its history. Any given point represents the complete state of knowledge about that system at a particular moment in time. So the picture is the picture of the movement of that point from one moment to the next. If a system is periodic, the point moves in the same loop forever. For example, in the system of the swinging pendulum, the strange attractor is the point in the middle of a spiral graph representing the steady state of no motion that pulls the trajectories inward as the pendulum loses energy to friction. But a strange attractor can be a trajectory toward which all the trajectories in the system converge (Gleick 1987, 137).

To retrieve a strange attractor it is necessary to embed the data in a phase space of sufficient depth. Systems with an infinite number of degrees of freedom require a phase space of infinite dimensions. A technique was developed for reconstructing the phase space from a flow of data, a technique that distinguishes between noise and chaos. In the new sense, "chaos" means orderly disorder created by simple processes. Chaos pulls the data into visible shapes and shows that, of all the possible pathways of disorder, nature seems to favor only a few (Gleick 1987, 266–267).

An example is the Lorenz Attractor. At any moment, the variables in a dynamical system fix the location of a point in three-dimensional space, and as the system changes, the movement of the point represents the changing variables. A simple example is the movement of a waterwheel: the wheel can turn slowly or fast or stop and reverse the direction of rotation depending on the flow of water. As the system changes, each moment can be represented by a point, and the sequence of moments is charted by connecting the points. After sufficient repetitions, what appeared to be random or chaotic motion begins to show a pattern of loops and spirals, revealing the presence of a hidden force or strange attractor. The loops and spirals of the attractor are infinitely deep, never meeting or intersecting. It is a distinctive shape, a kind of double spiral in three dimensions, like a butterfly with its two wings. In the case of the waterwheel, when the point moves from one wing to the other, it means that the wheel reversed directions. The shape signaled pure disorder, since no point or pattern of points ever recurred. Yet it also signaled a new kind of order. It revealed the structure hidden within a disorderly stream of data (Gleick 1987, 153).

The functions that produce the multiple scaling patterns are recursive, self-referential; the behavior of one is guided by another one hidden inside it. Lorenz's equations may help explain the erratic and inexplicable reversing of the earth's magnetic field as chaos within the geodynamo (Gleick 1987, 29).

The boundaries of strange attractors is a subject of immense interest, because they are the most unstable places, the places where "life blooms." The boundaries between two or more attractors in a dynamical system seem to be what governs many familiar processes, such seemingly unrelated events as the breaking of materials and the making of decisions. What is interesting is the way a system chooses among competing options, and thus how we might predict which of several nonchaotic final states a system might reach. Even when a dynamical system has non-chaotic long-term behavior, chaos can appear at the boundary between one kind of steady behavior and another. For example, in the case of the pendulum, which can come to a stop at either of two magnets at its base, each equilibrium is an attractor, and the boundary between them can be complicated but smooth, or complicated and nonsmooth. The system will definitely reach one of two possible steady states, but near the boundary, prediction is impossible (Gleick 1987, 233–235). Roger Lewin calls this boundary the "edge of chaos" where information processing is optimized (1992, 133).

Excitement about the unfolding of this new mysterious science can be seen in this statement by David Reulle, one of the discoverers of the strange attractor: "These systems of curves, these clouds of points suggest sometimes fireworks or galaxies, sometimes strange and disquieting vegetal proliferations. A realm lies there of forms to explore, and harmonies to discover" (cited in Gleick 1987, 153). And new laws of nature, new elements of motion also await discovery.

Mandelbrot identified two opposite effects in nature: the Noah Effect, meaning discontinuity, the possibility of a quantity changing almost arbitrarily fast; and the Joseph Effect, meaning persistence, the possibility of periodicity in nature. His point is that "trends in nature are real, but they can vanish as quickly as they come" (Gleick 1987, 94). One kind of behavior could be seen for a long time, but chaos shows us that this does not necessarily mean the behavior is in any way eternal; a completely different kind of behavior could be equally natural to the system. Climate could be like this: "The Ice Ages may simply be a byproduct of chaos" (169–170). Another possibility: The solar system looks stable, but it is conceivable that some orbits could become increasingly eccentric until the planets went flying off into space! (145) A more likely possibility is that humans are upsetting the delicate global ecology. By destroying the earth's cradle of life, the rain forests, which contains two-thirds of all living species, we may be destroying the evolutionary process and triggering a wildfire extinction in which we may be the first to go.

Now, this kind of thinking can give one pause. Even though experience may have given us many opportunities to notice this phenomenon, the power of our mythologies about reality tends to make us deny anything that doesn't fit. Our current worldview is built on the belief that what is is meant to be and permanent, and that progress is linear and predictable, onward and upward forever. It will not be easy for many people to give up this idea, especially those who perceive themselves to be doing very well with this paradigm. However, for those not invested in the received wisdom, women and other power minorities, for example, the new thinking may be amusing and inspiring—and empowering, certainly, for the human sciences.

Some say that twentieth-century science will be remembered for just three things: relativity, quantum mechanics, and chaos. They all undermine Newtonian physics: relativity has no abstract space and time, quantum theory has no controllable measurement process, and chaos has no deterministic predictability. Of the three, it is chaos which most impacts on the human scale of awareness of the world (Gleick 1987, 6).

Gleick says that chaos theorists feel that they are reversing a longstanding trend in science toward reductionism by looking for the whole rather than always analyzing systems in terms of their parts (5). Chaos is more than a theory; it is a method, a way of doing science (38), a new way of seeing. One way of accounting for nature is replacing another. Old problems are being seen in a new light, and other problems are being seen for the first time.

Robert May, a chaos scientist from biology, argues that every student should be taught chaos in order to counter the distorted view of the world that comes with a traditional scientific education. Chaos theory changes the way people think about everything from business cycles to the spread of rumors. May concluded that every aspect of life would benefit from the realization that "simple nonlinear systems do not necessarily possess simple dynamical properties" (cited in Gleick 1987, 80). I want to extend this revolution in thinking to education and the way people talk and think about the world and themselves.

Pattern formation is now a branch of physics and materials science, thanks to chaos, even though physicists were slow to accept the new theory. For instance, there is a new snowflake model that Gleick calls the essence of chaos. The snowflake is a paradigm example of the fragile balance between stability and instability in nature, representing the powerful interaction of forces across scales from the microscopic to the macroscopic which, from our point of view, produces an entity that contains the history of that interaction (Gleick 1987, 311). A snowflake is actually a "nonequilibrium phenomenon"; that is, a mere moment in the transfer of energy from one place to another (314).

The ultimate complexity may be the dynamical system of the human body, "a cacophony of counterrhythmic motion on scales from macroscopic to microscopic." However, there is no physical system that has been more obsessively approached from a reductionist point of view (Gleick 1987, 279). Now chaos is opening new doors. Physiologists are learning to see that health dynamics are marked by fractal structures; for example, the bronchial tubes in the lung and conducting fibers in the heart that allow a wide range of rhythms. Locking into a single mode prevents adapting to change, whereas nonlinearity in feedback processes regulates and controls systems; in a sense, chaos in the body's functions is essential for health (292–293).

Chaos may have important applications in psychiatry. Most accepted western scientific methods for treating mental disorders have been linear and reductionist, inadequate for treating disorders in the brain, the "most unstable, dynamic, infinite-dimensional machine" (Gleick 1987, 298). Some artificial intelligence researchers are using chaos in their efforts to model symbols and memory. A certain way of thinking about thinking suggests the chaos image of a phase space with basins of attraction, a model which seems to capture some of the characteristics of thought—impossible to pin down exactly, changeable, overlapping, attracting, repelling, etc. The fractal structure of the model seems to parallel the infinite self-referentiality that appears to be fundamental to the workings of the mind (Gleick 1987, 298). In the brain as in all dynamic systems, local interactions and emergent global structure are equally important and form a feedback loop (Lewin 1992, 191). Consciousness is part of the bigger picture of information processing that continuously produces increased complexity and structural changes in the brain, resulting in the emergence of properties at higher levels that depend on lower level activities (164). These insights are extremely important in understanding cognitive development, as I will show in chapter 5.

With or without chaos, serious cognitive scientists can no longer model the mind as a static structure. They now recognize a hierarchy of scales, from neuron upward, providing an opportunity for the interplay of microscale and macroscale that is characteristic of fluid turbulence and other complex dynamical processes (Gleick 1987, 299).

My interest in chaos is twofold. As a nonscientist I cannot claim to know much about chaos, but I understand some of the concepts at least well enough to see their power to affect some of the ways we think about reality; and these concepts support and expand the new paradigm of reality that has been developing in my mind and, I believe, in many minds. Also, the contemporary story of the making of a new science is certainly applicable to my discussion of creating a new paradigm for education based on a new paradigm of reality. An important part of my process of identifying a new paradigm of reality is taking concepts from many different disciplines and areas of thought as well as learning from the seemingly parallel paradigm shifts going on in many diverse fields—creating a cross-fertilization of ideas leading to a "supradisciplinary" paradigm.

The stories Gleick tells about the problems, predicted by Kuhn, that most of the pioneer chaos scientists had in getting others to take their new ideas seriously can serve to instruct and inspire those of us in a similar situation. We all know the truism that people basically do not want their bailiwicks disturbed, that they identify with their ideas to the extent that they feel personally threatened by any intrusions into or disruptions of their worldviews. But we do not experience the full force of this unattractive trait until we try to tell someone, particularly someone outside our own fields, that they have something all wrong. Gleick's account makes clear that the establishment of the science of chaos was hindered by the competitiveness and lack of communication and friendliness among disciplines, particularly physics and mathematics. In Russia, however, there is a strong tradition in chaos research dating back to the 1950s, marked by an atmosphere of disciplinary cooperation (Gleick 1987, 52).

It took many years, but finally, the unifying ideas of fractal geometry brought together for conferences and seminars many scientists from different fields who were having trouble understanding some problem they were working on, particularly problems that involved the way things meld, branch apart, or shatter, phenomena like the jagged surfaces of metals, and earthquake zones (Gleick 1987, 104).

There was a collective at Santa Cruz that for years did important pioneering work on chaos, completely out of step with the scientific community there. It appeared that they were bonded by a shared vision, the new realization that, when you step a little ways outside the physical systems analyzed by science, you enter a realm in which they don't apply. Some were philosophically satisfied to reconcile free will and determinism through a theory that contained order with emergent randomness and randomness with emergent order (Gleick 1987, 251).

Gleick says that the first chaos theorists "had a taste for randomness and complexity, for jagged edges and sudden leaps" (5). This may suggest that one must in a sense be constituted in a certain way in order to be receptive to the concepts of chaos. Those who like to play it safe within their closed circuits will probably not have a taste for chaos. Chaos is knowledge, and we have been taught that knowledge is power, but the knowledge of chaos seems to carry a message that we should be more humble, that nature will forever both seduce and elude us. The ancient mythologies seemed to know this, but modern science and technology have made us forget. There is little humility, irony, playfulness, or self-mockery in science, but Greek mythology, for one, abounds with it.

Scientists tend to talk about what they know as if it were all there was to know, as if only knowledge obtained through the "official" scientific method were real knowledge. The rest of society seems to pretty much go along with this idea; indeed, many critics and reformers in education seem to assume that the only goal is to raise test scores in math and science, because they believe that this knowledge is the only knowledge needed by society. But many of the pioneers in chaos are very influenced and inspired by poetry, music, and philosophy—and indeed, chaos contains a strong element of the poetic.

Also applicable is the thesis of Evelyn Fox Keller's book *Reflections on Gender and Science* (1985) that modern Western science is based on an ideological paradigm of patriarchal values and that it would be much healthier and more productive to replace this basis with a broader spectrum of concerns and attitudes, a fully human spectrum including both male and female elements. The new science of chaos seems to be an important step in that direction, as it breaks away from the ingrained thinking of traditional science.

My project of defining a new paradigm is about a new way of thinking. Therefore, it is important to investigate scientific knowledge about how the mind works. Happily, it appears that recent research in cognition and neural functions is quite compatible with the new paradigm. The new paradigm seems to fit the way the brain actually functions—a most remarkable fact, if it is true.

Erich Harth, in his book *Windows on the Mind: Reflections on the Physical Basis of Consciousness* (1983), emphasizes the importance of language in cognitive functions. We humans are held together by linguistic fictions that we believe. All of our separate needs, drives, and emotions are held together, if not quite unified, by the "verbal system." "It is language which, like a good interpreter, mediates between the different factions and sometimes, when the interpreter doesn't understand him [or her] self, makes up a story for the sake of harmony" (192). Harth agrees with neuroscientist Michael Gazziniga's conclusion that the mind is not a psychological entity but a sociological entity, made up of many "submental systems"; it is language that creates "a personal sense of conscious reality out of the multiple systems present," which produces the illusion of a unified self (192).

Like Bohm, from the perspective of quantum physics, Harth, speaking from the neurocognitive point of view, holds that subject and object mirror each other in a self-referential cycle. He quotes from Niels Bohr's "Biology and Atomic Physics": "The impossibility in psychical experience to distinguish between the phenomena themselves and their conscious perception clearly demands a renunciation of the simple causal description on the model of classical physics" (cited in Harth 1983, 226). Harth agrees with Bohm, Zukov, and others that if there is to be any understanding of the world or ourselves, it must be "grounded firmly on the premises of quantum mechanics" (222).

Calling it "the essence of reductionism," Harth disagrees with the theory that brain states are identified with specific sensations and are in principle determinable. Though some scientists believe that a device for accessing human thought is technologically feasible, Harth disagrees, saying incorrect assumptions are behind such ideas. The brain is a self-referential system that creates ever-changing images of "self" (1983, 215). This idea, coupled with the idea that one's verbal system constructs stories to make sense of experience, may be useful in analyzing the effects of being bombarded by disconnected images and ideas in the TV culture, as discussed in chapter 2. This knowledge also lends scientific support to the deconstruction of the concept of the subject and self that posits a unified consciousness, which will be discussed in the next chapter.

In studying the nervous system/brain/mind, says Harth (1983), we must replace notions of a rigidly ruled hierarchy of neurons with the notion of a "democracy" whose structure is heterogeneous and whose purpose is diffuse. We find more and more order because we look for it, but it doesn't follow that the brain or the universe is determined and mechanistic. Scientists don't look for that which cannot be ordered, but we should not conclude that there *is* nothing that cannot be ordered. This view parallels the Uncertainty Principle of quantum physics.

"The brain does not follow instructions, it simply *functions*." A computer is a closed system, the brain is an open system. There is a big difference. "Memory, motivation, associations— all the changes which in a computer would require instructions occur in the brain as a result of changes in the structure itself— the hardware" (Harth 1983, 232). "It is a paradox," says Harth, "that at a time when physicists find themselves unable to discuss the dynamics of the universe without involving human consciousness as a direct participant, materialist philosophers can still claim that mind is *nothing but* the 'mechanical *sprouting*' of a machine" (241). Harth says that nature is stranger than we used to think and believes it is naive to expect a machine to duplicate human cognitive functions, warning that "we must be careful when we replace things with what we believe are their equivalents" (231). Computer scientists in artificial intelligence should consider the neurological findings that problematize their agenda.

Harth (1983) believes that science will never be able to completely describe the human neural network, but that "a new vision, consistent with our deepening understanding of the human nervous system and the physical universe at large, will emerge slowly, probably after many more false starts" (155). He argues that every individual brain is unique and that every moment in a brain's life is unique. "Individual differences in the linkage between mental and brain states are expected to become more profound as we increase the detail in the description of the states. . . . Ultimately neither a physical nor a mental state will ever be repeated in all details" (239).

Already we know that the brain is a very plastic structure. Some regions seem to be "hard wired," but others, such as the cerebral cortex, are open to a variety of environmental as well as intrinsic influences. Some neurons have rigidly specified connections, and some are open to change under certain influences. It seems probable, explains Harth, that one learns by means of such modifications. Perhaps more understanding of the origins and process of thinking will one day be deducible from this kind of discovery.

Contrary to popular wisdom, there is a flaw in the body/machine, brain/machine analogy that makes the brain/computer analogy invalid. It is absurd to think of a thought from a brain without a body, because the dynamics of consciousness are almost certainly not separable from the dynamics of the world. Harth suggests that the boundaries of consciousness extend "well beyond the brain case, probably to the very surface of the body and even beyond" (1983, 101).

"Consciousness," says Erwin Schrödinger in his essay "Mind and Matter," is "the tutor who supervises the education of the living substance" (cited in Harth 1983, 202). "Thus," adds Harth, "my actions now may not be caused by my present consciousness particularly, but they are certainly guided by what I felt and thought in the past. Besides, I have at my disposal a verbal system which not only facilitates my access to past events, but also helps me to compile, correlate, and evaluate the past, and to project, simulate, and sample the future" (202).

Further showing the complexity of the brain, Harth explains that no single part of the cortex is necessary for conscious activity; it is a property of a very large system. It has been suggested that there can be no conscious response to a stimulus unless there is some type of neuronal reverberation lasting up to about one half second. But when sensation begins, the subjective judgment of its timing refers it back toward the time when the actual event took place. Sensations, then, are "replays of events that are well in the past, but manage to convey to us the delusion of a conscious immediacy and participation" (1983, 201, 202). I believe this is relevant to Derrida's deconstructive principle of *differance*, which I will discuss in the next chapter. Experiments have shown that a strong cortical stimulus can prevent conscious recognition of an earlier event (198). Data such as these might be useful in exploring the effects of television and TV culture on the mind.

Harth (1983) says that thinking and perceiving involve the same neural structures and work, perhaps according to very similar dynamic principles. A thought is a sensation that has substantial components of memory, projection into the future, and sensory or motor stimulation. "We thus erect a verbal structure around these phenomena and pretend that some identifiable physical reality is attached to them" (28).

The word "reflection" is a good description of thought, says Harth. "The cortex literally reflects, bounces back images that have impinged on it, producing new and modified inputs for itself. . . . The sensory pathways are not unidirectional but form loops whereby the stimulating, conjecturing, confabulating cortex can influence the stream of incoming information" (1983, 102).

"We can think of the fantasizing brain as attempting to wrest control over our perceptions away from the sensory input, while the senses keep the flow of imagination in check and anchor our perceptions in reality. If the anchor chain breaks, we are adrift in our dreams and hallucinations. If the sensory control is too powerful, our perceptions are dull, unimaginative" (Harth 1983, 159). If the image is sharply delineated, the perceiving mind cannot impose its whim on the received pattern; however, if the image is blurred, the mind is free to bend sensory reality to conform to its fantasy, the one most compatible with its reality. Knowledge such as this makes a valuable contribution to the study of the effects of media, especially television, on brain activity, and certainly seems to give support to those critics of television I discussed in the last chapter who warn of the dangerous effects of television, such as dulling of the mind and the confusion of the differences between fantasy and reality—a delicate balance in any case!

There is an interplay between senses and mind. What is sensed directly can be changed; elements may be replaced, distorted, emphasized, or repressed. Manipulation of some of the raw sense data is an essential component in the process of knowing. Without it, we would know nothing at all (Harth 1983, 163). Moreover, perception rarely involves just one of our senses. For example, the sensation of moving air is a blending of many senses. If any one of these were absent or distorted, our perception would seem bizarre and unreal because events are stored in memory as schemata, a structured combination of sensations, which are recalled when the same combination occurs, creating a feeling of familiarity that means "reality" to us (Harth 1983, 163, 164).

Such ideas about perception could, perhaps, make credible Baudrillard's extreme claims about media creating a "hyperreal" world in which all reality has been replaced by simulacra. Certainly, TV is very familiar to most people for these reasons, as I showed in chapter 2—*more* familiar than reality to many. In my own life, after I had been out of the country and away from TV for several months, watching TV became the most surreal experience imaginable. Moreover, American society seems surreal as it appears more and more to imitate TV. These ideas also problematize the increasingly popular notion in computer science that virtual reality has no limits, that computer-simulated experience can and will be indistinguishable from the "real" thing. This could only be true in Baudrillard's terrifying world where people had *already* lost most of their normal sense of what is real, and when we put two and two together, we can begin to see that this is all too possible, maybe even probable, maybe even already actual!

It is quite likely that the neural network with its 10 billion interacting neurons has some of the characteristics of a chaotic system. Brain behavior shows "a richness of form and an unpredictability that is reminiscent of turbulent flow" (Harth 1983, 211). There are rhythms that dominate, but there is always "massive and wholly unpredictable detail" (Harth 1983, 211). The microworld is inherently chaotic, but chaos, that is, unpredictability, also inhabits many macroscopic processes (204). We must become more respectful of the limitations our ignorance places on us when analyzing the microworld and, by extension, the macroworld. "The microworld of ceaselessly moving molecules provides fluctuations which in the case of the very delicately poised chaotic systems are sufficient to intrude on the world of large scale phenomena" (210). Perhaps thought processes resemble "a turbulent flow of information from the ministates into macroscopic neurodynamics" (213).

Thus, we see the science of chaos, a new paradigm of thinking, mirroring the mind that created it. Perhaps the science of chaos is the mind getting closer to explaining itself. Ironically and ambiguously, we can see simultaneous trends in what look like opposite directions: advanced technology is transforming and shrinking humans into sleeping, dreaming automatons, while at the same time, partly with the help of technology, many people are making tremendous breakthroughs that can expand and develop human awareness and experience and perhaps help us to break free from the horrible grip technology has on us.

Another move toward a new paradigm for thinking is apparent in Noam Chomsky's suggestion in *Rules and Representations* (1980) that it is time for a science of semiology that looks for abstract relations between disparate products and functions of the human mind, which may lead to a new cognitive psychology and theory of learning. Chomsky believes that there may be two separate but interacting systems: the system of computational rules and representations for language, and a conceptual system that links to the linguistic system but is also involved in nonverbal mental acts and processes. This notion may be compatible with brain hemisphere theories. Chomsky argues, in a fashion parallel to Harth, that what we normally call language might consist of different cognitive systems that interact in cognitive development. He says we won't get a unitary answer to the question "What is human language and how does it work." It is the wrong question (90).

Chomsky (1980) says that language should be studied as a natural science, that we should study the mind much the same way we study the body—as a system of mental organs, the language faculty being one, each having structure and function that are generally genetically determined. "Interaction with the physical and social environment refines and articulates these systems as the mind matures in childhood and, in less fundamental respects, throughout life" (241). Chomsky's view, like Harth's and Bohm's, departs from beliefs that are deeply ingrained in our intellectual tradition, based on "a belief in the accessibility, uniformity and simplicity of the mind" (241). People should let go of the accepted view that the human mind is unique among biological systems in its higher functions. Chomsky is convinced that the study of the biological basis for human language could be "one of the most exciting frontiers of science in coming years" (216).

An important balance has been lost in the minds of many who see only the scope and not the limits of human knowledge, argues Chomsky (1980). He believes that this unbalanced view is part of our cultural ideology. "There is no particular reason to suppose that the science-forming capacities of humans or their mathematical abilities permit them to conceive of theories approximating the truth in every (or any) domain, or to gain insight into the laws of nature. It might turn out, for example, corresponding to current theory in quantum physics and neurology, that inquiry into what humans do and why lies beyond human competence . . . a pessimistic conclusion, some might feel, but not necessarily false" (252). It is Chomsky's view that many scientists will not accept conclusions they don't like.

Sounding much like Harth, Chomsky says, "There is no reason to suppose that we have any privileged access to the principles that enter into our knowledge and use of language, that determines the form and meaning of sentences or the condition of their use, or that relate the mental organization of language to other cognitive systems" (1980, 244). Chomsky, like Harth, deals artificial intelligence a blow when he claims that "the study of grammar raises problems that we have some hope of solving, but the creative use of language is a mystery that eludes our intellectual grasp" (222).

Language is one of many complex mental structures that "arise under minimal exposure to the environment" (Chomsky 1980, 140), and so far, it is the most amenable to study. A major part of learning may be the growth of cognitive structures according to an internally directed course that is triggered and partially shaped by the environment (33). Therefore, "in certain fundamental respects we do not really learn language; rather, grammar grows in the mind" (134). "The mental faculty grows without choice, though not necessarily without effort or willed action" (140). In a sufficiently intricate structure, small changes at crucial points in development can lead to what appear to be different systems—for example, different languages. This idea is compatible with the idea in chaos theory of sensitive dependence on initial conditions, discussed earlier, that imperceptibly small factors can create large and significant effects.

Cognitive scientist Daniel Dennett agrees with Chomsky that "we have no direct personal access to the structures of contentful events within us" (Dennett 1978, 169). It is Dennett's project to develop a theory of consciousness "that can be continuous with and help to unify current cognitive theories of perception, problem-solving, and language use" (149).

He considers analysis of belief systems to be a vital element in studying human cognition, beliefs being more like fantasies, products of imagination, than like correlaries of experience. They are nonlinguistic, but they become "opinions" after language gives syntax and structure to them. Beliefs and desires predict behavior directly, whereas opinions can only predict behavior to the extent that beliefs and opinions are in rational correspondence. Only humans can act one way while judging another; this is possible because language allows for self-deception. Thus, many of the stories people make up to put the fragments of their experience together in TV culture may be quite maladjusted to their actual situations and/or contrary to their deeper beliefs.

Assent can be exacted so that one adopts a particular opinion, but this does not necessarily result in a corresponding change in belief. Beliefs are stronger and will win out or at least weaken the will. Normally there is harmony between our judgments and our behavior, and between our judgments and our beliefs, but it is possible for our sincerest judgments to be lies about our beliefs

(Dennett 1978, 49). Perhaps, to our great peril, it is now the norm to have lost this harmony between our judgments—our opinions and thoughts—and our beliefs, and we are suffering from this confusing psychic conflict.

These ideas could be very important to a critique of culture, thought, and language, raising questions about such things as the effects of media on belief formation. Dennett thinks people must learn to analyze their beliefs. They can do this, he says, by taking a "phenomenological approach" toward their own beliefs, that is, if people as phenomenologists view their beliefs as constructs instead of "real" objects, there is a chance that they will be led to alter them with discrediting evidence and reason (1978, 185).

In essence, people need to question their own authority about their beliefs; they need to see that beliefs have properties they hadn't recognized; they need to learn to suspend their beliefs long enough to analyze them and determine their value. Dennett (1978) says most people are already good at suspending *dis*belief; they will suspend disbelief to allow enabling assumptions for the sake of argument and forget later that the argument was dependent on this operation. But it is much harder for people to distance themselves from their beliefs in order to study them.

Another study shows that it is probably going to be much harder to realize Dennett's goal of belief examination than one might think. In their book-length study *Human Inference,* Richard Nisbett and Lee Ross (1980) present impressive evidence that people tend to cling to their beliefs even when circumstances change and their beliefs no longer match reality. They also provide some insights into the mechanisms that are responsible for belief perseverance.

They found no literature showing that people want to test their beliefs in order to discover and reject the ones that are unfounded. This does not mean that people never change their beliefs, but there will be less change than would follow from logical or normative standards, less than would result from an attempt to view the evidence in an unbiased way. As incredible as it may seem, studies show that people tend to keep their beliefs even when faced with proof that the evidence that initially produced the beliefs is wrong.

Nisbett and Ross attribute this irrational adherence to beliefs to the presence of higher-order goals; for example, having a stable belief system and saving time are two values that create cognitive dissonance when challenged by the suggestion that there is something wrong with what one believes, because it will be time-consuming, confusing, and disruptive hard work to analyze and correct the problem. It is better to put on blinders and defend the status quo. This may help to explain the findings of Yankelovitch, seen in chapter 2, that Americans were not letting go of their 1950s fantasies to face the harsh realities of today.

People sometimes have an emotional commitment to their beliefs, but persistence is likely even when there is no such investment because "a) people tend to seek out, recall, and interpret evidence in a manner that sustains beliefs, b) they readily invent causal explanations of initial evidence in which they place too much confidence, and c) they act upon their beliefs in a way that makes them self-confirming." The fact that people have such strong tendencies to persevere in their beliefs suggests that there are more basic and important goals than being correct. Nisbett and Ross pose these questions: Would people continue their irrational clinging to invalid beliefs if they better understood their behavior? And would their higher-order goals suffer if they did modify their belief-persistence behavior (1980, 192)?

Nisbett and Ross maintain that primacy effects in information processing are the rule, that is, early-encountered information produces theories that bias the interpretation of later-encountered information. This claim is important to the issue of the effects on learning and cognitive development of early childhood experience, including TV watching. Early evidence seems to create theories that are not sufficiently revised when conflicting evidence is presented later. "When people encounter probative evidence pertinent to prior beliefs they tend to apply assymetric critical standards to supportive and opposing evidence and tend to become more confident of a belief in response to a set of mixed evidence which normatively should serve to lower confidence" (1980, 192). That is, they will stubbornly persist in their old ways, seeing what they want to see regardless of the facts or even of the obvious failure of their methods of coping with reality. This is what the neoconservative education reformers, such as Hirsch, are doing, as discussed in chapter 1.

Nisbett and Ross (1980) show that beliefs have a profound effect on the way people make inferences; in a nutshell, beliefs prevent people from making logical inferences in every area of their lives. People have too much confidence in primitive judgmental heuristics and they pay little attention to conventional normative considerations. One of the main points of *Human Inference* is that people's theories about reality influence their thinking and behavior more than data do. The quality of people's inferences is at least as dependent on their psychological theories as on the data they have.

The problems of theory use, say Nisbett and Ross, are with the questionable origin of a theory plus misplaced confidence. "The informal store of haphazardly generated causal theory that each of us inherits is too facile and imprecise. An explanation of any given effect or its opposite usually is readily found by a little rummaging around in this bloated system" (1980, 119). In other words, if you want to justify yourself, you can always find an excuse to do so. For example, there are proverbs and truisms for every occasion: "he who hesitates is lost," but on the other hand "haste makes waste"; "absence makes the heart grow fonder," but "out of sight, out of mind."

It doesn't seem to take much to make people feel that they have some control over a situation when they don't. Nisbett and Ross give the example of people who had the chance to pick their own lottery ticket; they thought they had a better chance than did those who were just handed one. "Philosophers have long noted that people are often much too confident of their 'knowledge' and the accuracy of their judgments. Empirical research has provided evidence of this overconfidence and of the alarming extent to which confidence may often be completely unrelated to accuracy. . . . This seems particularly true of causal explanation" (1980, 119). One reason for this confidence is the ease with which one can come up with a theory. Unfortunately, one is likely to take the first theory that comes along and let it go at that.

A great deal of one's processing of information from the rapid flow of life's events depends on general knowledge of the world, much of which is represented as beliefs or theories, propositions about the world such as thinking America is the most altruistic country in the world, and schemata, scenario structures such as knowing what goes on at a university or how one is expected to behave in a restaurant or a movie theater.

The concept of schema is a cornerstone of modern psychological theory. It is widely accepted that "objects and events in the phenomenal world are almost never approached as if they were 'sui generis' configurations but rather are assimilated into pre-existing structures in the mind of the perceiver. . . . Unfortunately, the increasing conviction that schemata exist and are important has not been accompanied by a commensurate increase in our knowledge of them" (Nisbett and Ross 1980, 38). Not much is known of their properties, functions, or the conditions of their activation. We seem to have schemata, but there is a cost: they are easily overused and misapplied, misused when longer processes of judgment are warranted. It is clear that this is a vital area for study. Based on the sketchy evidence given in chapter 2, I surmise that mass media culture, especially TV, is implanting a multitude of maladaptive, contradictory, and confusing schemata into viewers' minds, particularly the minds of the young. One of the most harmful is the ever-popular scenario of good versus evil in which there are two unambiguously opposite sides settling the conflict with physical violence, which is always justified for the Good Guys. The beliefs of teenagers who unconscionably kill someone for fun or for Nikes, and of adults who gleefully support every U.S. military action regardless of the death, suffering, and destruction, are created and reinforced daily by endless versions of this scenario.

One example of faulty political judgments and policies that have resulted from misuse of schemata is President Johnson's use of the Munich Conference script to invoke the contrasting scenes of "the political compromise" in which one submits to an unprincipled power-hungry foe and "the military consequences" in which one gets run over by the enemy; this ploy was used to defend an aggressive and unbending foreign policy (Nisbett and Ross 1980, 39). Reagan used it, and Bush certainly used it in the Gulf War.

In 1843 John Stuart Mill described a bias he called "the prejudice that a phenomenon cannot have more than one cause.'' This has been supported by recent studies. Though people often say they recognize multiple causes, they seem to act as if they believed in unitary ''hydraulic'' causes (Nisbett and Ross 1980, 127–128). This attitude results from a kind of mechanical thinking. Studies indicate that when one believes there is an extrinsic motive for doing something, one behaves as though there is little or no intrinsic motive for doing it, even if she or he had had an intrinsic motive before introduction of the extrinsic motive. An example would be working only for money even though one used to perform the same activity for enjoyment. It has also been observed that people may use a causal analysis in one type of situation and not in another equally appropriate one, that is, there may be ''substantial compartmentalization'' of one's strategies (135), attesting to fragmentary thinking and a mechanistic worldview. One of the most common forms is the double-standard that keeps sexism and other forms of inequality alive.

Both laypersons and scientists, including social scientists, tend to commit the ''fundamental attribution error.'' That is, they hold the incorrect theory that human behavior is the expression of stable, predictable traits. They fail to see the power of situational forces operating at the time of action (Nisbett and Ross 1980, 107). This is relevant to the issue of the media's influence on people; it helps explain why people claim that they are not affected by, say, violence, sexism, or advertising on TV, in films, and so on. It is impossible to solve a problem when people don't even see the problem.

The dispositionalist/situationalist dichotomy parallels the mechanistic/holistic distinction. It is probably one of the main reasons mass media mind control is so effective while being firmly denied by most people. American ideology teaches— mostly, these days, through the media—that what happens to you is up to you; you are responsible for your own failures and successes. That this belief is probably essential in a capitalistic society, which must always blame the victim in order to deny its brutality, would explain why people ignore the vast amount of evidence supporting the situationalist view.

Studies show that vivid information that evokes imagery is emotionally interesting and has a greater impact on inferences than more abstract information, which has more probative and inferential value (Nisbett and Ross 1980, 45). One explanation is that it is easier to remember. Vivid information has more immediate impact than more abstract information, which produces more bits of information and takes more processing time; it is more likely to call from memory similar information, including schemata, because there are more access routes. This is bad news for those with complex and subtle ideas to convey. As Mander (1978) and Postman (1985) argue, TV is the perfect medium for imprinting the quick, spectacular, repetitive, and therefore lasting impression on the passive, receptive mind. The image is constructed to contain the message. Recently, there has been some interesting work done in an effort to formulate new theories of visual imagery in response to the predominance of imagery in contemporary popular culture. There is some discussion of this in chapter 2. Such studies will be invaluable to understanding belief formation and cognition in general and will be very important for education.

There is another problem of the fundamental attribution error. One can, for example, use the same terms for both actor and action: hostile actor, hostile action. There seems to be a linguistic bias in English against linking action and situation. And probably most important, studies show that people are susceptible to verbal manipulations through word choice and sentence structure when making causal attributions (Nisbett and Ross 1980, 122). A study of the effects of mass media on the American public can verify that. For example, a politically ignorant and naive public can be swayed to accept, even applaud, such military action as the attacks of the United States on Granada, Libya, and Nicaragua, and, most dramatically, the Gulf War, through media accounts that focus on the "democratic duties" of the United States rather than on the complex historical contexts. It is, therefore, essential to teach language mastery and rhetorical analysis as part of critical cognitive activity.

Another finding in the literature is that people usually make predictions that are inferior to those of actuarial formulas. It seems that probability information is used only in the absence of any other information. If people have any other information, even totally worthless information or misinformation, they will use it and ignore the probability information (Nisbett and Ross 1980, 141). Again, those who control mass media decide how the public calculates probability. For instance, because of the very few but highly publicized incidents of international "terrorism" involving Americans, millions of Americans fear traveling abroad, and during the Gulf War, even after it, many people wouldn't even travel to Paris or London. A more accurate picture is seen in statistics that show the United States to be the most violent nation in the world, with 10,567 handgun murders in 1990 compared with 22 in Great Britain (Austin *American-Statesman*, September 19, 1993).

One hypothesis in *Human Inference* is that inferential and judgmental errors arise primarily from nonmotivational sources (Nisbett and Ross 1980). Rather, errors result from perceptual and cognitive sources, which, of course, are often biased by motivational and emotional factors. The point is that many errors that are commonly attributed to motivational sources can be better understood as information-processing errors. It is very interesting that in our information age, so many people are so easily manipulated by misinformation and indifferent to the validity or sufficiency of their information. Baudrillard may be right—it's the more we are bombarded by information, the less we "know." Nisbett and Ross argue that the view that inference and judgment errors are caused by self-serving motivational factors is severely weakened by the evidence that these errors "often *undermine* self-esteem and *limit* the individual's capacity to satisfy personal needs" (1980, 13). In other words, when people mindlessly accept an ideology that is not in their best interest, they don't realize what they are doing to themselves and others by believing and behaving as they do. For example, many Americans believe they are safer if they own a handgun, but the fact is that this gun is forty-three times more likely to be used to kill the owner, a friend, or family member than to protect them. (Austin *American-Statesman*, September 19, 1993).

Nisbett and Ross talk about cost-benefit analysis involved in human inference. One of the ways ideology works is to trivialize or marginalize an issue so that most people won't think it is as important as other things and, therefore, won't spend much time, effort, or money on it. But the issues that seem insignificant are often vitally important keys to solving an important problem or complex of problems, as chaos theory makes clear. Therefore, teaching critical cognitive activity will be difficult because American ideology conveys the message that critical thinking ability and cognitive development and independent problem solving are not important; the American dream myth says nothing of such values.

In summary, then, it is *possible* to improve human inference, but there are big obstacles: (1) one's inferential habits cannot be directly observed, (2) the more important a personal judgment is, the more resistant one is to change it, and (3) one is usually too confident about her or his judgments to be interested in criticizing them. A critical mind will not produce a simple, predictable, safe, self-congratulatory worldview; therefore, most people would not want to develop that kind of thinking. The "commonsense" view is that the law of diminishing returns applies: you work hard and get nothing but worries and confusion; it is better to stick your head in the sand of delusion. Where is the Rambo of critical thinking? Who will teach us to eagerly seek disconfirmatory data, as John Stuart Mill exorts us to do in *On Liberty*—even if it means having to reject a proposition we hold to be true? Whose voices can convince us that there is a payoff?

New paradigms and discoveries in physics, chaos, neuroscience, cognitive science, sociology, philosophy, and many other disciplines can help to shape a new paradigm of reality to replace the mechanistic, reductionist, and static Newtonian model. Ultimately, assuming Postman (1985), Aronowitz and Giroux (1985), and others are right about the responsibility of education to lead in solving the problems we face, we must apply this new paradigm, this new worldview, to the formulation of a new paradigm for education that will facilitate the teaching of new, adaptive, enlightened ways of thinking. But insights into the human mind, such as Nisbett and Ross's studies on how people construct and live by their beliefs, worldviews, and problem-solving strategies, show that the stimuli presented to young minds have powerful effects that are difficult if not impossible to alter later. This implies that the potential for changing students' worldviews through teaching critical cognitive activity is severely limited. The new paradigm must be taught in the earliest formative stages of cognitive development. The following chapter is an attempt to further develop the paradigm, and the last chapter deals with the exigencies of cognitive development and education.

IV

Deconstruction

"You are always falling and catching yourself from falling; and that is how you can be walking and falling at the same time."

—*Laurie Anderson**

A new worldview requires a new mode of thinking. The mode of thinking that provides the condition for the possibility of a critical method that is suited for the exigencies of the contemporary world and that corresponds to and and connects the scientific theories and paradigms presented in the preceding chapter is deconstruction. There are many different and incompatible discourses on deconstruction, but my understanding and use of deconstruction is taken primarily from the originator of the term, French philosopher Jacques Derrida. In this chapter I will discuss the "concept" itself and how it applies to education, and in the next chapter, specifically how it can be applied to the teaching of critical cognitive activity.

Deconstruction is probably best categorized as a method and a practice. It is basically the reconceptualizing of thought, lan-

*From "Walking and Falling" by Laurie Anderson. © 1984 Difficult Music.

You construct intricate rituals which allow you to touch the skin of other men.

Photograph by Barbara Kruger, 1981. Used by permission.

guage, culture, and reality. It is the problematizing of the rigid categories and structures, based on language, that dominate Western culture. Deconstruction helps remove our socially conditioned blinders so that we may think and act more creatively and originally. It is not a brand new set of ideas; similar thinking has occurred throughout Eastern and Western history. And it is occurring today, in some sense, in many disciplines, as I tried to show in the preceding chapter. But it does go against the grain of institutionalized Western thought, and therefore many people resist or reject it, usually without much study or thought, because they feel threatened by ideas that demand changes in the way they think and act. Deeply ingrained unconscious beliefs about the world and ourselves are not easily dislodged, as I have already shown. But this is precisely what is now needed—the dislodging of certain feelings and assumptions that have become, if they were not always, dysfunctional.

The value of the deconstructive enterprise is that it enables us to understand more fully the structures of our reality—to play with them, change them, open them up to new possibilities—instead of being locked and smothered in them. Deconstruction tells us that our mental structures are semiotic in nature; they are constructed of signs, which do not simply represent reality, but constitute it. In other words, a thought or a spoken or written utterance is a new thing in itself, not just a vessel for a select bit of reality or experience. All signs "cut away" from their motivating references in such a radical way that the reference can never be completely or actually represented, or even proven to have existed, except insofar as it left the trace of the sign. Moreover, evidence was presented in the previous chapter that there is no exact referent; what we call a referent is an indeterminate chunk of experience constructed of more or less momentarily cohesive bits of data selected by a multitude of psychobiological processes.

It is this principle of cutting away inherent in the sign that Derrida calls *differance*; meaning is "deferred" temporally and "differs" spatially from experience, which is, therefore, always already absent from consciousness. Therefore, built on this shaky foundation, no constructed linguistic structure or system is a totally closed, complete, consistent, or true representation of reality. This concept seems completely consonant with the new scientific paradigm discussed in the last chapter.

Derrida has many terms for "difference," partly to elucidate the concept and partly to show the elusiveness of the concept, which he says is not quite a concept. "Differance" is the principle that operates the sign, which makes it the closest thing possible to a primordial and fundamental event underlying human thought and language—the "originary nonorigin of origin" (Harvey 1986, 166). "Nothing *precedes* it, nothing founds it, and nothing ultimately controls it" (159). Another word for "differance" is "trace." The movement of the trace is what constitutes both consciousness and the unconscious—the flux beyond the origin that allows for its constitution. As Irene Harvey puts it in her book *Derrida and the Economy of* Differance (1986), "That which forms its conditions of possibility, that which is the opening which necessarily exceeds it, are by definition not capable of being understood from within the same structure or system.... Structure as such, and language as structure, is prohibited therein from a certain omniscience. This prohibition is precisely the condition of its possibility" (130–131). I see chaos theory here. Language is a dynamic system. It is creative and unpredictable because it is at the edge of chaos (Lewin 1992).

Still another word for *differance* is "writing." Derrida uses the term "writing" to show that *differance* has the structure of graphic writing. His "writing" is a writing that *precedes* speech, then; that is, writing, or *differance*, is the condition of the possibility for the *spoken* word as well as the written word. This means that the "living speech," or even conscious but unspoken thought, of the "living subject" is not more "primordial than writing, or more proper," but rather that writing—*differance*—constitutes the condition of the possibility for meaning itself (Harvey 1986, 151). Language is a "subset of a wider notion of writing" (146).

Derrida " 'creates' his concept of metaphysics according to the problem of writing," says Harvey (1986, 98). That is, he critiques Western metaphysics as a "logocentric" system that depends on the truth of the "word" as an adequate representation of presence, consciousness, and transcendent reality. But, for Derrida, contrary to metaphysics, "the sign is irreducible.... The thing itself always escapes" (76). " 'Ordinary language' is always already installed within the system of metaphysical conceptuality" (110). That is, the way we speak in our own language, whatever it is, matches a certain way of thinking and processing the world, is created by this way of thinking, and perpetuates this way of thinking—whether we know it or not or want it to or not.

This does not mean that Derrida wants to abandon metaphysics. Indeed, he knows he cannot and that we cannot. Rather, he hopes to reveal and escape from the structure of authority and total unified meaning through *differance*, which has no power—is itself weak—but which "foments the subversion of all kingdoms" (Harvey 1986, 210) and guarantees that no one is able to own authority once and for all; it is always already up for grabs. Metaphysics and *differance* together produce "the play of the world"; that is, they provide the condition for the possibility of endless creative construction of structures about the world.

To use the chaos metaphor, deconstructive thinking is fractal thinking: a text is like a coastline, an infinitely long line in a finite area. If you look closer and closer, you keep seeing more bumpy coves. A text—any chunk of perceived reality you are isolating and looking at—isn't a transparent window on a chunk of thought any more than, as Mandelbrot said, mountains are cones or clouds spheres.

Practicing deconstruction is trying to critique the texts of oneself and others, to locate the "ruptures," to accept the ultimate "undecidability" of meaning. As Gayatri Spivak says, "we must learn to use and erase our language at the same time" (Spivak 1976, xvii). We have no choice but to use our language in interacting and coping with the world, but deconstructing as we go will help us realize the limitations of the tools we are working with and the consequent need for more receptivity, intertextuality, and creativity, and less rigidity, arrogance, and self-righteousness.

Deconstruction has important implications for teaching critical cognitive activity. Primarily, it can be an antidote to the current tendency in American society to think simplistically, and with great ethnocentric hubris, about complex old and new problems that involve the individual, the nation, and whole world. To break out of old, inadequate paradigms, it is necessary that people learn more of the nature of language in general and the biases language creates. Is it difficult to think deconstructively? No. Well, yes and no. No, because, if one is motivated, the fundamental ideas can be grasped more or less easily, depending on how they are presented; they can even seem self-evident, intuitively right, familiar. But yes, because practicing ways of thinking you believe in intellectually takes great effort if your conditioned ways of thinking are different. Also remember the disturbing hold our beliefs have on us discussed in chapter 3. And for the most part, we tend to think without much awareness of how we are thinking, so, like any new habit, thinking deconstructively, takes time and determination and self-analysis and self-criticism, and maybe a little help from your friends, but if you feel good about it and see effects you like, you will continue.

In his *Marxism and Deconstruction*, Michael Ryan (1982) explains his interpretation of Derridian deconstruction and its application to education. He argues that deconstruction concerns itself with how we conceive the world, which has great bearing on how we act. Essentially, it is a questioning of some major concepts and practices of philosophy. Basically, it shows the incompleteness of systems that have the illusion of absoluteness. Incompleteness and undecidability imply that all systems have a limit.

Though many American scholars, whether or not they have read any Derrida, have been persuaded that deconstruction is negative and promotes despair, meaninglessness, and chaos, I submit, as do Ryan, Harvey, and others, that for Derrida, deconstruction is affirmative. It can produce the thinking that could lead to the achievement of "togetherness of diversity," "difference without hierarchy"—a society free of nationalism, racism, sexism, homophobia, agism, or classism (Ryan 1982, 80). Deconstructive thinking is questioning middle-class philosophy, a way of thinking promoted by a desire for security that overlooks perplexing uncertainty and complexity.

Deconstruction is an aggressive act of reading that subverts the grounds of metaphysics in general and of idealism in particular. Metaphysics, Derrida shows, is not a historically periodizable school of thought; it is, rather, a permanent function of a kind of thinking that overlooks its own historicity, differentiality, materiality, and ties to language (Ryan 1982, 117).

Through the strategy of opposition and prioritization, metaphysics represses everything that troubles its founding values. Indeed, Derrida argues, its founding concepts—presence, ideality, and the others—come into being as the effacement and repression of such secondary terms as absence and difference. Deconstruction consists of upending the metaphysical system of oppositions and priorities by showing how what metaphysics excludes as secondary and derivative in relation to an originary concept of foundation—difference, say, in relation to identity—is in fact more primordial and more general than the metaphysical original. (Ryan 1982, 10)

Deconstruction wants to undo the inside/outside binary oppositions of metaphysics which promotes a set of chosen concepts that are opposite a set of rejected concepts. Easily recognizable examples are man/woman, good/bad, yes/no, us/them, white/black, god/devil, smart/stupid, rich/poor, capitalism/communism, and true/false. Deconstructing binary oppositions is a good place to start. It is easy for many people, I think, to see the point here. It is demonstrably wrong to think that the world is sharply divided into two classes of absolute opposites, one being superior, the other inferior. But it is easy to demonstrate the persuasiveness of such (non)thinking in our everyday lives. We are expected to identify ourselves as political liberals or conservatives. We are for or against capital punishment or abortion or drugs, and so on. Things are right or wrong. The answer is yes or no. You get the picture. The consensus of the establishment determines which side is good, correct, better than the other side. "America, love it or leave it." The underlying structure remains the same if the "bad" side appropriates it, as in "black is better than white, gay is better than straight." Deconstructive thinking is a way out of this vicious circle. It's the end of that game. It can enable us to avoid legitimating and perpetuating the structures that oppress us.

Metaphysics, it is important to realize, is not just an abstract subject confined to the philosophy classroom. Metaphysics is the ideology of social practice (Ryan 1982, 118). Derrida believes that the dominant "truths" of the world dominate primarily because they are favored by the powerful and forced on others, not because they are inherently superior ideas; that is to say, whoever rules politically gets to define, even construct, reality (Ryan 1982, 49). "Metaphysical thinking is important to ideology and to its function of legitimating dominance and guaranteeing hegemony because metaphysical thinking homogenizes contradiction, dissonance, and heterogeneity." Thus the deconstruction of metaphysics as the infrastructure of ideology must be an integral part of the critique of ideology (118).

Derrida says that the language of metaphysics is the only language available to use, so we "place it under erasure, effaced yet legible, so that it can be used against itself" (74). For example, we may use the accepted racial terms "black" and "white," but remind ourselves of the problems with these terms and try to replace them with terms that are less loaded with erroneous and negative sense, while remembering that all terms are just that— *terms*—linguistic constructs based on a trace of experiential referents. Deconstruction moves away from the universal meaning, truth, and essence of Western metaphysics and toward interconnectedness, relativity, and ambiguity. This move is rooted in the assumption that the world is a "texture of traces which exist as 'things' only as they relate to each other" (22). Moreover, ideas, concepts, truths, and meanings are only possible within the " 'cultural' institution of representation" (23). These notions are supported by the new scientific paradigm and new knowledge about how the brain/body functions to produce mind/consciousness, which was discussed in the previous chapter.

In "The White Mythology" Derrida argues, after Nietzsche, that all language is metaphor. "Metaphor might in fact name an actual state of things, characterized by transformation, alteration, relationality, displacement, substitution, errancy, equivocation, plurality, impropriety, or nonownership." Perhaps "impropriety is fundamental, [in] that metaphor founds language instead of being a derivative accident in relation to an absolutely univocal language" (Ryan 1982, 20). This means all terms and concepts are produced by metaphoric displacement; that is, they represent an always already absent, elusive, and ineluctible experiential referent composed of complex interactions of perceptions, thoughts, and processes that never really exist as a discrete, co-herent entity.

Consciousness, then, is inscribed, derivative, constructed, not the origin of ideal meaning and truth. Derrida shows us that consciousness is not the pure origin of meaning and truth about the world. It is a "text" composed by a complex weave of internal processes that are not and probably never will be completely understood. It is indirect and partial and delayed perception of reality from which we create meaning and truth, as Harth and others have shown from the perspective of neuroscience. Deconstruction implies that the world is not fragmented and categorized according to the structures of consciousness.

Neither Derrida nor Ryan write off conscious intentionality, the traditional privilege and center in metaphysics, but "situate it within larger structures and movements that allow it to function but deprive it of any empowering centrality or originality" (Ryan 1982, 32). The Derridian term "dissemination" is "the multiplicity of meaning that is not subsumable under a single paternal instance of authoritative conscious intention" (32). That is, the "author" cannot control where a discourse, spoken or written, will go or how it will be interpreted. This idea has created much furor in the academic community. It is seriously threatening to those who have built careers and identities on the proposition that one can and should be able to know what authors mean.

The deconstructionist teacher must claim that there is no strict inside-outside demarcation separating school from the world, no disinterested scholarship, no unbiased teaching. As Ryan puts it, "The fiction of an unbiased position is perhaps the most ideologically biased of all the possible positions" (Ryan 1982, 151). American education is a mode of social production that, from grade school to the university, determines how people think about the world and how they act in it. Deconstructionist teaching will critique the dominant ideology and allow for alternate interpretations of reality, not just replace it with a different one. Not that deconstruction isn't ideological—it is, but with a *differance* (pardon the pun). The difference is that deconstruction *exposes* ideology. It doesn't claim exemption as traditional ideology does. It claims to know something about language, thinking, and meaning which can make analysis more honest and complete. One can reach conclusions and make decisions (contrary to popular belief), but one must acknowledge their *limits*. The likes of Reagan/Bush melt into a little puddle like the wicked witch of the west if they can't claim total and absolute knowledge and understanding and control over everything. Everything. No wonder they hate deconstruction. No wonder Hirsch eschews critical thinking and cultural analysis.

Ryan points out that the division of academics into disciplines reflects metaphysical conceptual divisions and promotes ideological structuring of the social world. Perhaps the most dramatic example is the separation of economics and politics. These separations prevent people from making connections that might lead to a "revolutionary consciousness" (1982, 140). In the world, disciplines overlap and are never complete in themselves. It is not possible to analyze language in society without considering the political and economic uses of language. For example, the language of business implies a worldview which is reproduced through education in order to perpetuate the practices of the business world. "Language, then, is a material force in the reproduction of capitalism, more specifically, of the conceptual system which necessarily accompanies the structuring of the real world so as to serve the ends of capital" (141).

Deconstruction would question the conservative habit of thinking in terms of binaries, which makes a norm of their ideal model and treats everything else as a corruption of it. The business establishment wants academics to be loyal to the ideology of free enterprise, which they call "freedom." They can't afford to have this newspeak exposed. Deconstructionist teachers and business technocrats will necessarily clash over the role of the university in servicing capitalism, for business people are prone to repressing any teachers who threaten to expose their agenda. Business needs schools that teach that the nature of capitalism is good, natural, and self-evident; therefore, they do not want teachers who challenge this view.

Deconstructionist teachers will teach information that contradicts the version of reality constructed by conservative academic ideologues and the capitalist media, but not just information; to emphasize information will keep us in the abyss with Hirsch.

Information taught deconstructively is no longer information as we know it in the Western world. A different way of thinking changes the meaning of words as well as the meaning of the world. That is at least one reason some of the criticism against deconstruction sounds so rational to some people and so absurd to deconstructive thinkers. We aren't using words in the same way.

Moreover, I think deconstructive thinkers should come out of the closet and call themselves deconstructive thinkers. I think the "feminist" label argument applies here. So what if a lot of people scoff at the word—Fuck them! *We* know what we mean—more or less—and we should explain and stand our ground. To shy away from a perfectly good term seems cowardly and a waste of time, not to mention a way of avoiding the issue. For the sake of argument, we can say, Okay, *I* like it, so let's talk about the ideas it represents to me, which may or may not be similar to someone else's ideas. I certainly don't know everything everyone has said or written about deconstruction—or feminism—but I have put together some ideas from here and there that I call deconstructive and added my own.

I call my learned way of thinking deconstructive, and I call my way of teaching deconstructive. I have not, however, taught many students this term, but that is my goal—to teach in an environment in which it would make sense to do that, an environment in which there would be sufficient reinforcement.

Another American scholar, Frank Lentricchia, makes an argument similar to Ryan's in his book *Criticism and Social Change* (1983). He says, too, that teachers must work on exposing the ideology of advanced capitalism and encouraging cultural revolution. He sees American critical theorist Kenneth Burke as the antidote for the ills in our educational institutions. Lentricchia says that, though most avant-garde thinkers ignore Burke, he anticipated both structuralism and the critique of structuralism, poststructuralism. For over fifty years, his aim has been to "work toward the undermining of the sociopolitical order in dominance, and, in the same gesture, to assist in the birth of an emergent society" (86). (There's that concept of emergence again.) In 1935 Burke proposed that the substance of ideology is discovered through texts, the rhetoric and mythology of society (24).

Burke's work should be seen as an effort to "explode the myth of disinterest." He wants to show that intellectuals operate "within the larger capitalist project whose purpose is always to prepare the sheep for market" (Lentricchia 1983, 88). Burke wants to expose all the subtleties of the hegemonic process in order to broaden the consciousness, to prepare for a new kind of praxis—an enabling, connected feeling of social responsibility that will make us whole, integrated people with more control over our lives and society than we can have with traditional liberal ideals.

For Burke, intellectual activity is very necessary in society's power struggles, but most intellectuals, claims Lentricchia, consider themselves outside of, even above, such struggles. Lentricchia says that Burke's first principle is that all intellection is a form of political action as well as a form of rhetorical action, the key word being "action." Burke calls literature "equipment for living" and Lentricchia asserts that "all literary power is social power" (Lentricchia 1983, 19). He says teachers of literature should ask themselves if their teaching will enable their students to cope with problems in the real world and to reread culture from the perspectives of the oppressed and excluded.

Lentricchia (1983) charges that traditional teachers of literature politically tranquilize themselves and their students by their passive presentation of the literary canon as the ahistorical unified voice of literature. They do not see their role in suppressing cultural heterogeneity. For Burke, literature and art in general help create our sociopolitical nature; aesthetic theory is social theory. Art is not apart from the world; it is oppositional activity in the world, a discordant and disruptive voice out to undermine any one particular structure of reality. This view is also argued by Jean-François Lyotard in *The Postmodern Condition.*

In teaching, Lentricchia says, we must realize that literature or any text will exert no power over the student if there is no overlap in ideology. The student will be uninterested and will not react politically to a text if he or she cannot in some way identify with it. Such identification necessitates a sense of history without which one cannot understand one's culture, and must therefore be, willing or not, an agent of the status quo disqualified as an agent of social change. Today's educators are up against the horrifying reality that most American young adults are decidedly lacking in a sense of history, if we can believe the surveys that report that a majority of high school students do not know when or why the Vietnam War was. On the twentieth anniversary of the Kent State Massacre, I asked a class of twenty-five university freshmen what had happened and showed them the famous newspaper photograph that appeared that morning on the front page of the *Boston Globe*. Two students knew what had happened, one only vaguely. Moreover, most of them didn't seem very interested in finding out. One student made the solemn pronouncement that these people had, after all, broken the law. This is only one of many examples I or any teacher could give. In this state of ignorance, how can young adults begin to critique current U.S. foreign policy, or see the need to?

According to Lentricchia, the various "priests" of hegemonic society, such as TV and school, educate the socially dispossessed to feel that they have a stake in the authority structure that dispossessed them. They feel that their only hope of repossession lies in their allegience to the structure that has dispossessed them because they do not see any alternative. An alternative is exactly what I, Burke, Lentricchia, Ryan, Derrida, McLuhan, Postman, Aronowitz, Giroux, and others of like mind want teachers to provide. People need to learn that any group can appropriate the linguistic symbols of authority and create their own language of possibility; Burke calls it the "stealing back and forth of symbols" (cited in Lentricchia 1983, 79).

Burke anticipated Derrida in describing the "essentializing strategy of interpretation," which explains the complex in terms of the simple by singling out one motive as the essence of reality, with all other motives seen as corruptions and variations of it. Burke's concept of the "god-term" or "ancestral term" reveals the genealogical will to power behind the essentializing impulse and, therefore, all systematic thinking. Against this essentializing impulse, Burke encouraged, as Derrida does, a "playful" strategy of interpretation that allows the complexity, undecidability, and the radical heterogeneity of reality. Burke deconstructs systems of thought and terminologies, including his own, without destroying the humanistic impulse inherent in his "dramatistic" theory of human activity, which revolves around his "pentad"—

act, scene, agent, agency, and purpose—the five aspects of linguistic behavior (cited in Lentricchia 1983, 71–72).

Another educator who is developing the educational implications of Derrida is Gregory Ulmer. In his *Applied Grammatology: Post(e)-Pedagogy from Jacques Derrida to Joseph Beuys* (1984), Ulmer discusses Derrida's concern about the effects of the electronic media on education and argues that intellectuals can no longer ignore the radical cultural transformation now in progress. There must be a new discourse for those continuously exposed to film and TV (265).

In 1976 Derrida addressed the Estates General, urging teachers to study and use media, for, he said, it is within the media that the battle for influence would be fought. The concern of the Estates General was with "the functioning of the marketplace, the techno-politics of the 'media' and with what the government administers under the name of 'culture' and 'communication' " (14–15). Ulmer asserts the point that McLuhan and others have thoroughly argued (which was presented in chapter 2) that the dominant communication medium directs thought, and he therefore concludes that a new cognitive style is emerging in the electronic culture; the relation of speaker/writer to discourse is changing, as well as the way one communicates with oneself. Derrida, like McLuhan, has investigated the shift in the ratio of the senses, though Ulmer points out that before either of them began their studies, Gaston Bachelard said in the 1930s that the new physics rendered conventional thinking in philosophy obsolete. He said that a new pedagogy would be required in order to reeducate human sensibility at its root. Thinking with conventional logic would no longer suffice. Ulmer thinks, as I do, that the theoretical fictions of new science might inspire a pedagogy that would merge the concepts of teaching, research, and art and would help transform society.

Derrida was active in a group called GREPH, which formed to address the issue of teaching philosophy in the public schools. GREPH firmly opposed the Hegelian pedagogy that defines the teacher's role as model and authority and privileges verbal discourse. Contributing to this dialogue in their analysis of education as an instrument of class power, Pierre Bourdieu and Jean-Claude Passeron say that traditional professorial discourse "prevents learning, alienates the student, and condemns the teacher to theatrical monologue and virtuoso exhibition even while maintaining the fiction or farce of dialogue" (cited in Ulmer 1984, 172). Indoctrinated teachers believe they can only repeat already established conclusions, and people accept this as natural. Ulmer, too, sees a caste of intellectuals who ensure hegemony. Education legitimates the authority of the state and reproduces the nature of society. And the system works because teachers misunderstand the ideology of academic freedom and the illusion of autonomy. They are the faithful transmitters of a tradition and not the transformative intellectuals working toward a philosophy in the process of formation.

Ulmer's main point in his book is that pedagogy needs a paradigm shift. He says that part of Derrida's analysis of writing in general is an analysis of Western pedagogy. Edward Said says Derrida's enterprise may be essentially a pedagogy, while others say Derrida rather encourages others to formulate and practice a deconstructionist teaching method. Derrida says: "Deconstruction has always had a bearing in principle on the apparatus and function of teaching in general" (cited in Ulmer 1984, 159). Rather than focusing on deconstruction per se, though, Ulmer chooses to work with Derrida's concept of "grammatology" in his search for a new pedagogy. Harvey defines "grammatology" as the science of writing, invented by Derrida and built on Nietzsche, Freud, and Heidegger. Grammatology keeps alive the unresolved contradictions of language, constantly questioning the authority of the "logos"—the law—and deconstructing the privilege of the spoken word (Harvey 1986, 50).

Ulmer wants to identify the pedagogical principles of applied grammatology. This will require a move beyond conventional pedagogy toward a pedagogy for the age of electronic media, a discourse that is at once popular and learned. We must ask what kind of education is adequate to a poststructuralist epistemology and a media-dominated society. Ulmer says that the fundamental difference between the old pedagogy and a new one would be a shift from "truth" to invention. The classroom should be a place of invention—production, rather than reproduction (164). An open pedagogy will expose the traditional "prestructured predigested product designed for consumption

Photograph by Barbara Kruger, 1982. Used by permission.

by a homogeneous group." Pedagogy will become *process*, not product (307).

Teachers must look for open models that allow change, growth, and "the vision of a universe founded on possibility" (Ulmer 1984, 308). Ulmer believes that applied grammatology can have power beyond deconstruction "to stimulate the *desire* to create, not necessarily in art, but in the lived, socio-political world" (264). I believe that Ulmer and I are in basic agreement about the power of deconstruction in the new pedagogy, but I prefer, for now, to stick with the term "deconstructive thinking" which for me, in combination with the other aspects of the paradigm as I conceive it, entails everything Ulmer means by his term. In the open pedagogy, form is a range of possibilities from which one chooses, final meaning being, as Derrida says, "undecidable." Ulmer (1984) explores the verbal images of discourse for the possibility of inherent meaning and explores TV and the computer as things and vocabularies to be compared to the semantic fields of cultural studies (314–315).

Ulmer believes that grammatology should involve film and video theory and practice. Perhaps audiovisual media should move to a primary role in education to accommodate the shift in thinking modes brought about by filmic structuration. One may be able to learn from visual as well as verbal codes if visual media are used for new purposes that are suited to their strengths. Film, for example, is not just a medium for telling stories; a montage of images can produce a concept. Familiar images can be recombined to create new concepts or deconstruct old ones. Ulmer cites McLuhan's *Gutenberg Galaxy* as a major representative of postcritical writing, with its borrowings and verbal collages. He defines postcritical writing as any writing—graphic or nongraphic or a combination—characterized by the use of the collage/montage method as a device for deconstructing logocentrism.

Transformations in education must take place before students can be taught postcritical writing. I believe that the steps I have outlined so far are essential in the project to effect these transformations. We must begin with a critique of the state of contemporary education, as I outlined in the introductory chapter. Then this critique must be placed into the larger picture of a critique of the state of our contemporary culture, which I attempted in the second chapter. But before we can fully critique either education or culture, we must have a theoretical basis for our critique.

A great deal of what is wrong with education and culture is attributable to the prevailing worldview, the traditional Newtonian worldview based on the static, linear, mechanical, reductionist model of modern Western science. To break out of this worldview into a bigger, more realistic and liberating one, we must construct a new one. I outlined in the third chapter what I perceive to be the new paradigm of reality that is actually taking shape by putting together many ideas from different sources and fields, ideas that appear to me to fit together, to be parallel paradigmatically and to inform each other. I focused on the sciences because that is where I happened to see dramatic paradigm shifts occuring.

There is a bit of a problem here, because precisely what we do not want is a paradigm dominated and determined by the white male elitist Western traditional scientific ideology. Indeed, Kuhn (1970) and others in their analyses of paradigms and paradigm shifts often seem to imply that these issues are relevant only to science. Feyerabend (1975) is an exception, with his desire to learn from all ways of knowing and to be "against method," adopting a free "dada" attitude against the constraints of society, but his ideas are not very well known. Not surprisingly, it is his more conservative student Kuhn who has been more readily accepted.

But, as I see it, the paradigm shifts going on in the various sciences are a move *away* from the white male elitist ideology. I see this most dramatically in the new science of chaos. In fact, chaos can be a very effective and evocative metaphor for our new paradigm of reality, because it breaks away from the old scientific paradigm in precisely the ways that I want our new paradigm of reality and our new paradigm of education to break away from it; at least, it breaks away on some poetic level that can be snatched before it is appropriated by the scientific establishment.

Unfortunately, many of the scientists now using chaos theory are probably still thinking in terms of the old worldview, the old

paradigm, outside of their scientific work. It is a big philosophical and cognitive leap to a truly new way of thinking. Those
who do not make the leap will make any new ideas fit into their
old structures of thought. Ahead lies the most difficult task.
What mechanisms are involved in transforming a person's and
a society's ways of thinking, their basic belief systems? How do
you change the way people view the world, themselves, and
their relationship to the world and each other? I don't know. But
we must try to find out, and that is what I am working on, as
are many other people from many different perspectives. I hope
all of us will come together eventually—soon—just as the very
diverse chaos pioneers eventually found each other and put their
ideas together after years of working separately against the grain
of the work that everyone around them was doing.

What I present in this chapter on deconstruction are the ideas
that I believe to be the essential basis for a new paradigm of
society and a new paradigm of education, education for critical
cognitive activity. I believe the set of ideas I am calling "deconstruction" is a link between the new directions in the sciences,
particularly chaos, and the everyday world, the world of the
liberal arts and the social and political sciences. Deconstructive
thinking is a new way of thinking for most of us. It is the way
of thinking of the new paradigm of reality and the new paradigm of education. I believe it is the way of thinking behind the
scientific paradigm shifts. As Gleick (1987) notes in his book on
chaos, it took a particular kind of thinking to create and appreciate this science in the first place.

Chaos may teach science new ways of thinking, but to some
extent, one must already think in certain ways that are similar
and compatible—for the most part, one must have an open
mind. Some minds cannot be opened. But some can. Many
minds can open if a key is provided, and I believe that the more
one is exposed to new ways of thinking, the greater the chance
that one will eventually be transformed by them. I believe that
for our society to adopt a new paradigm of reality, individuals
must, one by one, become deconstructive thinkers. If this is going
to happen, I believe that the new paradigm for education must
be deconstructive in nature.

Deconstruction produces a new kind of truth and meaning,

just as chaos produces a new kind of truth and meaning. We need the new linguistic and conceptual tools provided by these theories and practices. Deconstruction, as a critique of reason, the rational and logic, that is, Western science and metaphysics, is fertilizing Western thinking; likewise, chaos, says Gleick (1987), is fertilizing Western science. Perhaps it is not an exaggeration to say that chaos and deconstruction can put the life back into science and society.

Of course, all of these steps are simultaneous, recursive, and interconnected. I have been learning, experiencing, and observing in all these areas for many years, and what I think in one area affects the way I see another area. If I didn't know how to think deconstructively, I would not be making this particular analysis in this particular way, so for me, deconstruction is the intellectual key to the project of constructing a new paradigm of reality that can be the basis for a new paradigm of education.

---------------------------- **V** ----------------------------

Critical Cognitive Activity: A New Paradigm for Education

"You connect the dots."

—*Laurie Anderson**

In my investigation into the well-established problems of our society and the education system, which was prompted by my professional interest in teaching writing, literature, and critical thinking to college students, I was led to the discovery of harmful cultural influences on our students, especially the intellectually stifling TV entertainment ethos that currently dominates our culture. I believe these influences are not often fully recognized and dealt with effectively. I concluded that to date, both liberal and conservative reform measures and proposals are failing to address the real need of students preparing to live in a democratic society, namely, the need to be taught by socially active intellectuals to develop a language of possibility, one with which they can think, read, write, and act in the best interests of self and society.

I summarized E. D. Hirsch's neoconservative theory of cultural literacy, which in many ways is antithetical to my own, and ar-

*From "Sharkey's Day" by Laurie Anderson. © 1984 Difficult Music.

gued that it does not address the most crucial factors involved in literacy problems and education problems in general. It is my position that both the literacy problems and the concept of cultural literacy are much more complex than Hirsch acknowledges, and, more important, I attribute the problems in education to structures and changes in American society, not simply, as Hirsch attributes them, to a faulty "liberal" education theory that is preventing the school system from giving students the education they need. In contrast, I presented Stanley Aronowitz and Henry Giroux's analysis and critique of American education and their agenda for radical reform as a guide for others to follow.

I have shown through a wide variety of sources that American culture, in some ways, produces maladaptive behavior and that the American public has difficulties coping effectively with the contingencies and exigencies of contemporary life. Yankelovitch and others show that Americans tend to value their own personal freedom and economic opportunities without understanding the political, economic, and psychological realities that impinge on that freedom and those opportunities.

Winn, Postman, Mander, and McLuhan show how the pervasive influence of TV in American culture, which is constantly promoting unbridled consumerism, is having a deleterious effect on cognitive and emotional development in children, especially those who lack strong parental guidance. Postman and McLuhan, as well as Aronowitz and Giroux, Ryan, Lentricchia, Ulmer, Derrida, and others, give educators the primary responsibility for emancipating people from the grip of the dehumanizing forces of the electronic age. We believe it is essential that education include instruction in critical thinking, and specifically in critical awareness and analysis of TV and technology as well as their ideological influences. We all see the absorption of the individual into electronic culture as threatening the end of the possibility of participatory democracy, which requires the involvement of mature individuals capable of understanding complex social issues.

Many of the thinkers presented in the previous chapters are calling for a new worldview, a new model of the mind, a new paradigm of reality, and a new paradigm for education in order to orient ourselves effectively to the problems of contemporary society in the electronic age. Just as the current worldview can be represented by the machine model of Newtonian mechanics, the new emerging worldview can be represented by chaos theory, which stresses relativity, ambiguity, chaos, uncertainty, and connectedness rather than the absolute truth, objectivity, order, and predictability implied by the old mechanical model.

I argued that the project of finding a new paradigm for education must be informed by the paradigm shifts and new knowledge to be found in various sciences. Particularly since a new paradigm is a new way of thinking and because teaching requires understanding of how people think and learn, I presented some of the recent research in neuroscience and cognitive science. One especially important insight is that, though the computer has become the popular metaphor and simulacrum of the human brain, showing the persistence of the old paradigm, neuroscience research is increasingly proving the brain to be nonmechanistic, self-referential, chaotic, and inaccessible. In other words, it is not much like a computer at all. Most important, it is constantly changing with higher properties emerging from lower ones.

Nisbett and Ross, Dennett, Derrida, and others show that a worldview is based on unconscious mental processes and beliefs that people are reluctant to identify, challenge, or change, even in the face of compelling evidence and even though those beliefs were usually acquired only because they were presented chronologically first and thus never really chosen at all. Mander and others argue that TV is one of the major, if not the major, source of these mental processes and beliefs; it is the machine that is installing and implanting them. If a new, more effective worldview is to be constructed, then educators must be able to reach the unconscious minds of students in order to influence earlier cultural conditioning, which has already instilled a language, belief system, ideology, and worldview and is being strongly reinforced day by day. They must be able to effectively teach ways of seeing, analyzing, critiquing, and changing the traditional and current influences and patterns of thought, feeling, and opinion. Eventually, one hopes, children will be taught about the world with the new paradigm from birth by parents, educators, and

society in general, but for now the emphasis must be on transforming the way students think and, consequently, behave—a
task daunting in the extreme.

The previous chapter presented deconstruction as central to a
new paradigm for education. I cite Ryan, Lentricchia, Ulmer, and
Derrida to help explain the relevance of deconstruction to the
classroom. We agree that it should be used to teach a new, productive way of questioning, knowing, and problem solving that
questions all the accepted assumptions, categories, and arguments of society. A deconstructive paradigm would emphasize
creativity, criticism, and heterogeneity over the absolutist static
order of the old paradigm and would emphasize process and
development over product and information, thus promoting a
new worldview. As one way to accomplish this, Ulmer has suggested postcritical writing—the production of provocative montages of texts designed to generate creative thoughts that will
penetrate the unconscious.

To implement the deconstructive paradigm of critical cognitive activity, we need a theoretical framework in which to place
society and the individual, learning processes, thought, and language. We need a theory that will incorporate the principle that
developing the intellect is a form of social and political action as
well as rhetorical action, a theory that can expand to accommodate new knowledge and the new paradigm, a theory of the
processes, development, and relationships of thought and language, individual and society. The theory of Soviet cognitive
psychologist L. S. Vygotsky is such a theory.

VYGOTSKY'S THEORY OF THOUGHT AND
LANGUAGE

Vygotsky argues that the problem of thought and language is
the focal issue of human psychology in society (Vygotsky 1962,
xxi). In *Mind in Society*, an edited edition of Vygotsky studies,
the four editors state that Vygotsky's "legacy in an increasingly
destructive and alienating world is to offer through his theoretical formulations a powerful tool for restructuring human life
with an aim toward survival" (Vygotsky 1978, 133). He joined
anthropological and sociological studies with observation and

experiment in "the grand enterprise of accounting for the progress of human consciousness and intellect" (14). In his introduction to *Thought and Language* (1962), Vygotsky's seminal work, Jerome Bruner says that Vygotsky gives a historical perspective to the development and nature of thought, and also proposes a mechanism for becoming more free of one's history: Vygotsky's theory is a "description of the many roads to individuality and freedom" (x).

One of Vygotsky's primary claims is that thought develops from the social to the individual, that is, the relations between individuals in society are the foundation for all the higher functions in the individual. Furthermore, Vygotsky posits the thesis that intellectual growth is socially coded, contingent upon mastering language, the social means of thought.

Thinking and language development and usage involve the entire material culture; the nature of the development of inner speech and verbal thought changes from biological to sociohistorical. Vygotsky says, "All higher functions are not developed in biology and not in the history of pure phylogenesis. Rather, the very mechanisms underlying higher mental functions are internalized social relations. These higher mental functions then become the basis of the mature individual's social structure. Their composition, genetic structure, and means of action—in a word, their very nature—is social. Even when we turn to mental processes, their nature remains quasi-social. In their own private sphere, human beings retain the functions of social interaction" (cited in Zebroski 1983, 55). It follows, then, as I argued in chapter 3, that individuals will tend to mirror the characteristics of their society in their thinking. And without very special intervention, they certainly will. Note the catch-22: one needs the right social environment for healthy development of the individual, and one needs to have healthy development in order to create the right social environment! Therefore, we, now, must suck water out of a rock and pull ourselves up by our bootstraps. If the mechanisms underlying higher mental functions are internalized social relations, then it is not difficult to see from the evidence we have that these mechanisms are not in good working order in today's developing minds and, therefore, cannot perform the necessary functions in the evolution

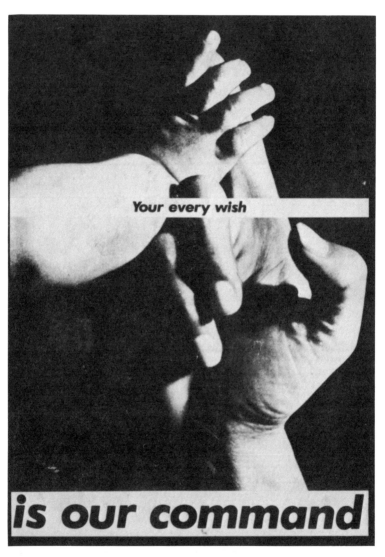

Photograph by Barbara Kruger, 1981. Used by permission.

of cognitive abilities in the development of critical cognitive activity.

The subject/object split in Western society that makes a distinction between personal experience and objective reality has created an education system that requires students to detach themselves from what they study, as shown in previous chapters. At the heart of Vygotsky's theory is the conviction that satisfying personal needs and adapting to reality are not separate or opposite. Satisfying a need entails adapting to reality. Adaptation is always directed by needs (Vygotsky 1962, 21). This implies that the first task of the educator is to determine accurately what students need.

One of Vygotsky's main contributions to psychology and education is his conception of development. Vygotsky saw development as natural, as a phenomenon in which all things are in motion and internally contradictory—"a complex dialectical process"—a dynamic system in the sense of chaos theory. He states: "The connections among developmental stages that interest us in child psychology are dialectic. Each successive stage in the development of behavior is the negation of the preceding stage" (cited in Zebroski 1983, 64). It is negation in the sense that the qualities peculiar to the first stage of development are copied, destroyed, and sometimes transformed into a higher stage. This may be a key to understanding the lack of higher stages of cognitive ability. We may be able to analyze an individual's stage of development and discover where her or his progress was arrested, then to know what training is needed to continue development. I believe the current situation in culture and education retards the developmental process of many individuals. They have not been able to achieve higher levels; they are handicapped with the inadequate features of a low level of cognitive ability. As chaos theory shows, the brain only has emergent properties at higher levels that depend on lower level activities (Lewin 1992, 164).

The Soviets generally consider dialectics as a theory of knowledge and cognition, something of a metaphysics subject to deconstructive analysis, but it is more useful in a process model than the static binary oppositions of Western metaphysics. Vygotsky's view of the dialectic is the opposite of the method of modern Western metaphysics as defined in the previous chapter. "This method postulates that, in reality, all objects and phenomena are intrinsically interconnected and interdependent, that all of them are inherently contradictory, and that due to the struggles of opposites they undergo constant changes and pass to a higher qualitative state" (Zebroski 1983, 69).

Vygotsky's claim that society is the main source for individual development of higher mental processes and that development consists of many levels that are interconnected and in constant flux are two propositions that are very important to the study of the development of language, or, to use the term Vygotsky prefers, "speech activity." There is no exact equivalent in the United States to the theory of activity that is central to Vygotsky and Soviet social sciences. It roughly corresponds to "cultural behavior." The study of any activity must consider its context in an individual's life; that is, its connection to other activity. "Activity" is similar to what some contemporary cognitive psychologists call "schema," as seen in chapter 3. It is a "framework of implicit assumptions and expectations generated by society within which actions and operations are carried out" (Zebroski 1983, 89).

The dominant or "leading" activity is the activity that leads the individual into a new developmental stage. The nature of the leading activity will be different across culture and history, because it depends on the tasks and problems that are relevant within a given social environment. Therefore, the leading activity should be the basis of all teaching, because teachers must always be able to discover methods that can create bridges to advance students from what they can do already to what they cannot yet do, to new activities that are necessary to functioning outside of school. This advancement to more challenging activities is parallel to achieving higher stages of cognitive development. Thus, every subject should be taught, not as detached from social and personal life, but as part of a natural process closely interconnected with general contemporary social and personal life as well as the student's unique social and personal life.

I have surveyed classes on this matter and found students overwhelmingly reporting almost no connection between school education and the exigencies of daily life, except for extracurricular activities attached to the student life-style. Such surveys, are, in fact, a potential leading activity. Discussing the issue can lead to student-generated proposals for school structure, policy, courses, and suggestions for activities in the class, as well as activities outside of school that can supplement formal education. Students can relate to this activity, and if they take to it, there is no end to the work that can evolve—an infinitely variable multifaceted project of group and individual thinking, speaking, listening, writing, critiquing, reading of written and visual texts, information gathering, and so forth. Clearly, the traditional textbook will be of little use, as I will discuss later.

The ultimate aim of education, according to Vygotsky, and I agree, is to promote the development of consciousness, awareness and control of one's thoughts. The ability to direct one's thoughts is, to a great extent, especially in early development, socially acquired. Therefore, if society and education present no tasks, make no demands (other than obedience and memorization under threat of punishment), fail to stimulate a child's intellect by providing goals and the proper sort of assistance for reaching them, thinking will not reach the highest stages, will not be *conscious* thinking. The dynamic system of the brain will not transform in ways necessary for the emergence of consciousness. Development occurs in interaction with instruction, but they are not parallel, and their relationship is very complex. Instruction usually precedes development, but there may be no perceivable development for some time, and then there may be a sudden leap in development. Vygotsky stresses the importance of discovering the hidden processes of development so educators may design instructions more appropriately.

An important concept in Vygotsky's activity theory is the "zone of proximal development." It refers to the student's potential to do more than she or he can already do if given sufficient assistance. It signifies a higher level of accomplishment that the student is on the verge of reaching but has not yet reached; therefore, it is closely linked to the leading activity, for the teacher can plan effective instruction only with understanding of the student's potential. Such instruction will focus on what a student can do and build on strength instead of trying, usually unsuccessfully, to build on weakness.

Moreover, there is a sensitive period when the student is most ripe for learning, most receptive to a particular kind of instruction. For example, Maria Montessori discovered that young children of four or five "take" to writing in a way that older students rarely do. So it seems clear that in redesigning education with a new paradigm, it is important to pay attention to not only what and how students should learn, but when.

Activity is characterized by change, and a primary focus in Vygotsky's theory is on the changes that occur in speech activity (language), notably the transformation of speech as it becomes internalized and becomes what is called "inner speech." Analysis of inner speech is one of the Vygotskian school's major contributions and an essential concept for the formation of a new paradigm of critical cognitive activity, because it is necessary for educators to know how speech and thought development work.

"Inner speaking" is subvocalized speech, but inner speech is unspoken and unconscious; it is highly condensed and is the structural opposite of outer speech and written speech activity, "a kind of abstract of speech which . . . is a copy or abstract of the 'world' " (Vygotsky 1962, 132). As a person forms linguistic habits and repeats a certain verbal structure that is more or less the same with each repetition and carries more or less the same meaning, a condensed, synthesized version forms in a sort of unconscious linguistic reservoir, as it were, which the speaker draws from in future instances and also adds to and modifies by future use. Over time, a particular verbal structure will become more deeply rooted and will consist of a network of nuances, images, variations, emotions, and other associations that have been part of the experience in which the verbal structure was uttered, heard, read, written, or thought. We can quickly see that the kinds of experiences the individual is having are all important. We can also quickly see that the kinds of experiences common in our TV culture must be affecting inner speech formation adversely.

Vygotsky makes a distinction between the "sense" of a word and its "meaning." The sense of a word (or larger verbal structure) is more important in inner speech than its meaning. The sense is all the individual psychological associations that have become the subjective meaning of the word, whereas the meaning is the culturally shared, more stable referent. Though shared meaning is important, subjective sense has much more power over the individual and can change within and vary among individuals almost without limit. It is important now to remember the critique of Hirsch in chapter 1 and see more fully the implications of his emphasis on shared meanings as the glue of society and his neglect of anything more complex, personal, and rich.

It is inner speech that one draws on most when thinking, speaking, and writing. When a verbal structure from inner speech comes to consciousness in response to a particular situation, one must give it full shape to fit the conventions of the particular context—the activity—if is to be expressed. And what one is attempting to do linguistically must be in one's zone of proximal development; that is, there must be something in inner speech for the new experience to connect to. If the speech or writing or listening is performed effectively with conscious effort and interest, it follows that one is increasing language mastery. Inner speech is thereby enriched through a feedback loop process, since it is performance and perception in the first place that create inner speech. To the extent that one has successful experiences in speaking or writing with clarity, subtlety, style, sophistication, simplicity, and other effective characteristics, speech activities, at least of the types an individual is used to, will become qualitatively better and easier to perform.

Therefore, since speech activity is closely linked to cognitive development, it follows that a primary goal of education under the new paradigm must be to expand and enrich inner speech. Though everyone's inner speech is uniquely his or hers and, therefore, not exactly like anyone else's, most inner speech is not original or unique to the individual. Rather, it is taken from the social environment of the individual; therefore, most of what a person internalizes is copied, mimicked, imitated. Generally, an individual's inner speech is a mirror of the ideas, conventions, and ideology of society. According to Vygotsky, *one cannot develop cognitively as an individual separate from society until advanced thinking processes are learned.*

The formation of inner speech is a kind of inner programming; beneath consciousness there is a sediment of thoughts, beliefs, feelings, and associations that form the basis of our conscious thoughts. *This cannot be ignored by educators.* Inner speech theory illuminates many of the failures and problems of today's education system, notably the chronic problems of low verbal skills such as writing, reading, speaking, listening, and thinking. Many educators may realize that we are now an image-oriented TV culture, but they probably don't know very much about how this is affecting students in terms of how they think, what they think, and how they learn, though there is increased interest in constructing theories of imagery. Within a paradigm of critical cognitive activity these factors can be more realistically confronted.

Vygotsky says that inner speech is intimately connected with written speech activity. The structure of inner speech activity is very important for a theory of writing. Writing is not just inner speech made outer. It is a "transformed form" of speech, "a complex product of a profound and involved development in the realm of inner speech" (Vygotsky 1962, 139). For one thing, writing, being so much slower than outer or inner speech, creates the possibility for a new kind of inner speech, new, richer developments in thought. To write, one must have skill in abstract deliberate activity, because the progression from compact inner speech to detailed written speech is long and difficult; and for this process to be understood, writing must be placed in the context of other social activities.

This view of writing supports a thesis that the poor writing of students is linked to their lack of cognitive development, which is also social development. If writing draws on the reservoir of unconscious inner speech, the individual's internalized thoughts, students can explore and expand the depths of the reservoir through precise written articulation of what they think, learning to critique what they think, and discovering new ways to think. Teachers can establish a positive feedback loop between writing and thinking that will be invaluable throughout students' lives. Writing forces an intense dialectical relationship between inner speech and conscious outer expression, which is usually more focused, organized, and developed than informal verbal or nonverbal expression because one can have time and concentration, in privacy, when writing. These insights shed light on the true nature of the problem of inadequate writing skills. It isn't simply the lack of a skill which can be taught in isolation. Nor is it realistic to think that a semester or two in college of freshman composition can produce dramatic results. In a sense, what we are asking of teachers of such courses (who are usually under-trained and underpaid) is to bear the entire burden of the failures of society and the education system!

A major premise of Vygotsky's theory is that, though the relationship of thought and speech undergoes many changes, both phylogenetically and ontogenetically, progress in thought and speech are not parallel; their growth curves cross and recross, merge, run side-by-side, and diverge like two rivers. But they should not be considered as separate. Thought and speech unite into what Vygotsky calls "verbal thought," and the smallest unit of verbal thought is word meaning (Vygotsky 1962, 4, 5). Vygotsky argues, deconstructively, for the existence of a dynamic system of meaning in which thought and language interrelate, but without forming a unity.

Vygotsky posits that initially thoughts are nonverbal and speech is nonintellectual. At first, very young children parrot the speech of others without associating it with specific meaning, and since they don't yet know language, their mental activity does not take linguistic form. Soon, though, from the intrusion of culture and innate biological development, thought and speech become fused; children are attaching thought to language. But in both children and adults, this fusion is limited to a circumscribed area. Nonverbal thought and nonintellectual speech continue to function apart from this fusion and are affected only indirectly by the process of verbal thought. The usefulness of such an insight is an awareness that thought and language are not correlated in any simple way, that all utterances are not necessarily the product of the speaker's thought, and that a student may have varying difficulties in articulating thoughts, depending on the nature of the thought.

Speech shapes thought processes, and writing probably shapes thought processes even more because more effort is involved, and words undergo an evolution of meaning. For a long time words seem to children to be attributes, properties of objects, rather than signs. A series of complex molecular changes lead to the critical realization of the internal sign-referent relationship.

The sign or word is the "means by which we direct our mental operations, control their course, and channel them toward the solution of the problem confronting us" (Vygotsky 1962, 56). Moreover, Vygotsky deconstructively problematizes the word when he says that the meaning of a given word is approached through another word, and whatever we discover through this operation is not so much a picture of the person's concepts as a record of the relationships in the person's mind between previously formed families of words. Also, a word is a generalization, and generalization is a verbal act of thought that reflects reality quite differently from the way sensation and perception reflect it.

Vygotsky does not privilege the word as an unmediated window on reality: "All the higher psychic functions are mediated processes, and signs are the basic means used to master and direct them. The mediating sign is incorporated in their structure as an indispensable, indeed the central, part of the whole process. In concept formation [the highest level of mental activity in Vygotsky's hierarchy], the basic sign is the word, which at first plays the role of means in forming a concept and later becomes its symbol" (1962, 55). Further problematizing the process, it is necessary to add Derrida's deconstructive notion, which I believe is implied in Vygotsky's theory, of the trace structure inherent in the sign (that the referent of the sign is nebulous, fleeting, and always already absent from signification, leaving only its trace), making absolute meaning ultimately undecidable. Those who attempt to teach critical cognitive activity need to be aware of these complexities inherent in cognition, language, and writing.

Vygotsky brings all his ideas together in his analysis of the development of verbal thought to its highest level, concept formation. Concept formation is not merely association; it is an aim-directed process, a series of steps toward a goal. For the process to begin, a problem must arise that can only be solved through the formation of new concepts. According to Vygotsky, concept formation is a higher-order cognitive skill that is acquired gradually by a series of essential steps. Children's concepts differ markedly from adults' in composition, structure, and mode of operation. After children learn to generalize, they begin to learn to abstract, but the first step toward concept formation is not obvious as such because the child abstracts a group of characteristics without clearly distinguishing one from the other; often this type of abstraction is based only on a vague, general impression of the objects' similarity. Still, the global character of the child's perception has been breached. An object's attributes have been divided into two parts unequally attended to, the beginning of positive and negative abstraction. An object no longer retains all its attributes; some are denied admission. The object is impoverished thereby, but the attributes that are picked out acquire sharper relief in the child's thinking (77). From now on, the child's thinking is shaped by the attributes that the culture deems significant, and reality is no longer perceived holistically; it is constituted.

At first it is impossible for the child to separate the field of meaning from the objects in the world. But later, the child's language becomes capable of talking about something other than what is there (Vygotsky 1978, 97). A split between the fields of meaning and visualized objects occurs at preschool age. In play, thought is separated from objects, and actions stem from ideas rather than things; for instance, a piece of wood becomes a doll, a stick becomes a horse. Action according to rules begins to be determined by ideas and not by objects themselves. This is such a dramatic reversal of the child's relationship to the real, immediate, concrete situation that it is hard to imagine its full significance. This shift occurs over time, not all at once; it is very difficult for a child to sever thought from object. But once accomplished, a person's verbal thought need never again correlate with the "objective" facts of reality; the ground is set for cultural ideological and religious abstract structures, which produce beliefs, superstitions, convictions, purposes, and actions based on others' interpretations of reality rather than individual interpretations of experience. Perhaps watching TV for hours on end from infancy interferes with this natural process. If cognitive development results from challenging and meaningful tasks, then it may be incalculably detrimental to development to put children in an environment that deprives them of interesting tasks and problems to solve requiring imagination and resourcefulness, such as making toys, inventing games and activities, and exploring and discovering the natural and the cultural environment.

Vygotsky links the development of higher mental functions with the formation and application of concepts—verbal thought structures. He describes the stages in the process of this development. It is essential that teachers understand these stages if they are to contribute to the mental development that is fundamental to critical cognitive activity.

Before real concept formation can occur, the child develops a distinctly different thinking process, which Vygotsky calls "complex" formation. The principal function of complexes is to establish bonds and relationships. Complex thinking begins the unification and organization of scattered impressions; organizing discrete elements of experience into groups creates a basis for later generalizations. But the advanced concept presupposes more than unification. To form such a concept it is also necessary to abstract, to single out elements, and to view the abstracted elements apart from the totality of the concrete experience in which they are embedded. In genuine concept formation, it is equally important to unite and to separate: "Synthesis must be combined with analysis. Complex thinking cannot do both. Its very essence is overabundance, overproduction of connections, and weakness in abstraction" (Vygotsky 1962, 76, 77). We must ask how the developing mind can even think in complexes in front of a TV screen with disconnected and meaningless images flashing into it through the eyes at the rate of two or three per second.

The pseudoconcept predominates in the child's real-life thinking and is an important link between complex thinking and concept formation. Vygotsky calls this "incoherent coherence" of child thinking (and, I would add, of a common childlike thinking in adults) "syncretism." This phenomenon is the result of a tendency to compensate for the lack of understanding of the relationship between things by making too many subjective connections and mistaking them for objective connections (Vygotsky 1962, 60). TV culture, as defined in chapter 2, tends to arrest cognitive development by promoting this primitive level of thought, through its fragmented, shallow, and incoherent nature, epitomized by TV, which may hold the viewer's mind in this mode or the mode of Vygotsky's "complex" thinking, or even some mutant mode, subverting any attempt to move beyond with the ceaseless and rapid generation of fragments.

Since at first the child incorporates different things into a group on the basis of concrete imagery, there is a constant struggle within the developing language between conceptual thought and primitive thinking in complexes. "In the contest between the concept and the image that gave birth to the name, the image gradually loses out; it fades from consciousness and from memory, and the original meaning of the word is eventually obliterated" (Vygotsky 1962, 74). "The primary word is not a straightforward symbol for a concept but rather an image, a picture, a mental sketch of a concept, a short tale about it—indeed, a small work of art. In naming an object by means of such a pictorial concept, one ties it into one group with a number of other objects. In this respect the process of language creation is analogous to the process of complex formation in the intellectual development of the child" (75). In both, the abstraction is shaky and weak and easily lost in the presence of distractions. But, later, when concept and word-forming ability has strengthened, meaning is not so easily lost.

A complex cannot rise above its elements as a concept does; it is a fusion of the general and the particular. Vygotsky observed in his extensive work with mental patients that thinking in complexes is characteristic of schizophrenics, who regress from conceptual thought to a more primitive level of mentation rich in images and symbols; concrete images instead of abstract concepts is one of the distinctive traits of primitive thought. Thus, the young, the primitive, and the insane, says Vygotsky—and I will add those who are products of TV culture, though their thought processes may differ in other important respects—all manifest this trait: relating objects or phenomena that have no contiguity or recognizable connection, so that partial identity or close interdependence is established. I believe it is primarily this manner of perceiving reality that has generated the schizophrenia, confusion, alienation, numbness, and violence in today's society, as well as the postmodern sensibility.

Once one has developed the higher-level thinking skills of concept formation, it is necessary to add the skills of deconstructive analysis to comprehend the Babel of postmodern discourses and to destabilize select concepts that have become too rigid or narrow and to produce new ones. In a sense it is arguable that deconstructive thinking, which has some of the properties of thinking in Vygotskian complexes, is a level of thinking higher than conceptual thinking. It may be the emergence of a higher level of consciousness, which is, in effect, the new paradigm of thinking. This line of thinking as well as Vygotsky's entire theory of development seems to fit the ideas of chaos theory and neuroscience (presented in chapter 3) that emergent properties of the brain appear from lower level activities.

It is not until adolescence that Vygotsky sees full-blown concept formation evolving. He studies the intrinsic bonds between external tasks and development dynamics, and finds concept formation to be a function of the adolescent's total social and cultural growth (Vygotsky 1962, 79–80). The conception of word meaning as a unit of both generalizing thought and social interchange is invaluable to the study of thought and language. It provides a basis for study of the relationship between the growth of thinking ability and social development.

No new basic function appears, but all the existing functions are incorporated into a new structure, form a new synthesis, become parts of a new complex whole; the laws governing this whole also determine the destiny of each individual part. Learning to direct one's own mental processes with the aid of words or signs is an integral part of concept formation. Analysis of reality with the help of concepts precedes analysis of the concepts themselves; thus, it is often difficult for adolescents to explain the concepts they use and difficult for everyone to express concepts which are new to them. Perhaps more difficult is applying a concept to new concrete situations; this step may be as difficult as the earlier one, moving from concrete to abstract thinking. Also difficult is the creation of new concepts and the deconstruction of concepts, which requires thinking that is, at least to some degree, independent of the assumptions and conventions that formed the concepts in order to keep alive the dialectical relationship between complex and concept.

One of Vygotsky's most important findings is that development of higher thinking processes based on concept formation must occur in stages and that direct teaching of concepts themselves is impossible, resulting in empty verbalism, which only simulates a knowledge of concepts and covers up a vacuum. It seems obvious that most traditional educators take no account of such ideas, thus rendering most teaching ineffective on these grounds alone. The empty verbalism of, say, Hirsch's cultural literacy or any rote memorization of subject matter is, indeed, a simulacrum in the Baudrillardian sense.

Moreover, this development is nonlinear and the cognitive functions involved in learning different subjects are interdependent; they all facilitate the learning of the others and combine into one complex process. Learning conscious control over one kind of concept results in automatic restructuration of all the other concepts the individual knows, says Vygotsky. One is not bound by one system, but can switch at will from one to another, transcending structural bounds. For example, Vygotsky distinguishes between the "scientific" concepts learned in school and the "spontaneous" concepts learned from life experiences. Ultimately, scientific and spontaneous concepts, though they develop in reverse directions, move together. The upward growth of scientific concepts toward increasing abstraction and the downward growth of experiential concepts toward increasing concreteness are connected processes that facilitate each other (1962, 107–109). I take this to mean that in a healthy learning environment, all learning would be integrated to the extent that ways of thinking and knowledge learned in one context would transfer to and enrich the different ways of thinking and knowledge learned in a different context. For example, being able to move easily back and forth, consciously and perceptively, on the concrete-abstract continuum is helpful in any thinking task. However, what Vygotsky may take as the normal course of cognitive development does not appear to occur in our society, even, as Nisbett and Ross (1980) point out, in the privileged thinking of scientists.

Vygotsky's project and mine, however, is for society, particularly though not exclusively through the education system, to provide the conditions for the possibility of individuals to develop the higher-level functions. Understanding the process by which this goal can be accomplished with Vygotskian theory, and all the cognitive research that expands it, as part of the critical cognitive activity paradigm can help us see where in our society the breakdown in this series of steps is occurring. Vygotsky's theory makes it easier to see that, as Winn (1985) and others argue, a TV culture as defined in chapter 2 necessarily tends to retard the development and thus prevent the maturation of individuals and society. The retardation occurs mainly because TV culture is based on technological interference with meaningful interaction of the individual with other people and the environment which Vygotsky argues is essential to development. Moreover, as we saw in chapter 2 TV mentality encourages the reduction of complex issues to simple and distorted formulations, thus subverting the perception of the need for understanding and development of higher mental functions. There is already a shocking number of people who say cheerfully that reading and writing are becoming obsolete. Within the context of TV culture, Hirsch's theory of cultural literacy further legitimates this mentality.

TEACHING "WRITING" AND CRITICAL COGNITIVE ACTIVITY

Throughout *Thought and Language* (1962), Vygotsky stresses the critical importance of the social environment on the developing mind, particularly the tasks society gives people, especially children, to do. I have argued that many people in American society today are significantly lacking in what Vygotsky calls the higher mental functions, even though they are products of the school system. I am led to the conclusion that the advanced concept formation processes that are essential for effective problem solving, surviving, and living in today's problem-ridden society are not being sufficiently developed; the "radical change in the intellection process" is not occurring as it should. Moreover, some aspects of modern American culture disrupt and prevent the development of advanced thought and language, thereby crippling overall development of the individual and society. Nothing is more crucial than analyzing this situation and plotting strategies for correcting it.

Since I have designed, developed, and taught, in the United

States and abroad, many writing courses of all types at university undergraduate, graduate, and professional levels and courses in literature, philosophy, critical thinking and global culture with writing components, I have a particular interest in composition pedagogy. I have come to believe that it has a central role in this enterprise because the development of writing skills is interwoven into the development of thinking and verbal skills. We must understand what is happening in the development and see where the breakdown is occurring, and then design a new composition pedagogy based on Vygotsky's theory.

Vygotsky claims that such early and seemingly unrelated activities as make-believe play and drawing are all moments in a basically unified process of the development of written language. This suggests that Marie Winn's negative assessment of typical contemporary child development in *The Plug-In Drug* (1985), discussed in chapter 2, has some bearing on the writing inadequacies of college students. Therefore, in order to understand literacy as well as cultural literacy and cognitive development, such technological intrusions into the growth process as television and the computer, in addition to the social structure itself, must be analyzed for the part they play. In this way, teachers of critical cognitive activity may understand the mechanisms of the social trends responsible for retarding students' development and, therefore, more effectively challenge those trends.

I am opposed to the current practice of teaching writing as a technical skill rather than as an essential tool in cognitive development, and I place teachers of writing at the center of emancipatory reform in education because they can develop students' capacity to think conceptually and critically through mastery of language. But if teachers of writing are to take an active, leading role in institutionalizing the new deconstructive paradigm for education that will effectively address the problems of today's students, many changes must be made in the way they think about teaching writing.

Writing and teaching writing must be reconceptualized in the context of the academic curriculum. The new paradigm will challenge the very structure of the composition course within the curriculum. *Writing must be put in its place.* Within the new paradigm, teaching writing is not just about teaching writing. It is mostly about other things: It is about teaching "writing"—Derrida's deconstructive principle, which underlies and produces all signification. It is about promoting the critical study of culture; it is about developing students' thought and language skills; it is about the "writerly" reading of texts; it is about putting chaos in the classroom.

I want to argue that there should be no more separate composition courses. In fact, I don't want to use the term "composition" because it smacks of the dull traditional concept of teaching students to imitate a set of models and follow the rules. Instead, there should be a multitude of courses in which critical cognitive activity will be taught and encouraged. There should be writing components in courses throughout the curriculum that are designed to facilitate teaching critical cognitive activity in connection with the course subject matter, and schoolwide writing centers that offer assistance in the technical aspects of writing. The current trend toward writing-across-the-curriculum programs should evolve into critical cognitive activity–across-the-curriculum programs.

Only this kind of deep-structure reconceptualization will produce the changes in education required by today's world. It is not enough for writing specialists to carry the mechanics of writing from discipline to discipline; this only reinforces the old order. And we don't need just a new "order"; we need a dynamic system, an open structure of chaos/order. It must carry the supradisciplinary deconstructive paradigm of thought and language in order to broaden the minds in every discipline with critical cognitive activity. And, of course, all educators in all areas must incorporate the new paradigm however possible and restructure courses and programs accordingly.

The old composition paradigm tends to treat language as capable of unambiguous expression of thoughts generated by autonomous apolitical subjects. The goal of the writer under this paradigm is to produce clear meaning by imitating models of writing that have been legitimated by the various institutions of society. This goal can certainly survive in the new paradigm, and should, for students do, indeed, have practical writing needs; but this goal will be subsumed under the larger goal of critical cognitive activity, which questions the meaning and validity of these models in a cultural context while simultaneously promoting their reproduction when warranted by a critical analysis of a particular task. Again, the chaos model applies: depending on what your interest is in something, you may see order or you may see chaos; the recognizable patterns of order may disappear as you look closer and closer, and they can even reemerge as you look still closer. Therefore, for certain tasks traditional patterns may be quite applicable, but our deconstructive vision shows us the fuzzy edges where they begin to break down and makes us more aware of their constructed, sometimes arbitrary, nature and the possibilities for flexibility and new patterns.

Reproducing, revising, and replacing the accepted models of writing from a viewpoint expanded by cultural analysis, chaos theory, cognitive science, deconstruction, and Vygotskian theory is a necessary part of developing the language of possibility, which I see as the goal of emancipatory education. Students must be able to use the conventions of language effectively and critically if they are to actively and creatively participate in the activities of society. Deconstruction is necessary to the new paradigm because it problematizes meaning and language in a way the old paradigm does not, and Vygotskian theory is necessary because it draws attention to the process by which individuals construct language, the centrality of language in society, and the role of language as a social force that constructs the individual's mind.

In addition, flexible theories of teaching composition that have been successful under the old paradigm should be adapted to the new paradigm. James Kinneavy's (1971) theory of discourse is well suited for adoption because it can be creatively adapted to provide students with a dynamic model of the components of writing and the spectrum of aims and modes that writers encounter in real-world writing tasks. Kinneavy's theory helps the writer select the conventions and strategies appropriate for the intended reader and the particular purpose of the writer. His model can give structure to writing assignments designed to give students practice writing a realistic variety of texts with a variety of topics, readers, aims, and modes that approximate as closely as possible the exigencies of real-world communication and when possible writing in real world situations while advancing the interests of the student and the projects of the course.

If TV is the symbol of what is wrong with contemporary American culture, writing is the symbol of the solution; writing is at the core of the new paradigm for the electronic age. Derrida's "writing," or "*differance*," as the trace of that which is not present, well represents the postmodern age of Baudrillard's simulacrum, in which meaning is finally exposed as having no origins except the opening and closing of electrical circuits. But at the holistic end of the spectrum, Vygotsky's inner speech theory, supported and updated by current research in the neurocognitive sciences, leads to a hypothesis that, literally, writing is the antithesis of watching television. TV implants (writes?) thoughts and images into the unconscious and inner speech of the passive viewer, whereas writing engages the active intellect in retrieval and conscious formulation and manipulation of thoughts from inner speech and also enriches the writer's reservoir of inner speech with new verbal thought.

Vygotsky says writing requires abstract thinking and goal-oriented concept formation in the process of converting inner speech to fully articulated utterances and creating new inner speech. Therefore, it follows that writing is an act of resistance, defined by Aronowitz and Giroux as exertion of power against the dominant power structures that "write" on us and program us through mass media. Writing is resistance against the effects of our TV culture, which subverts our mental and social development. Writing activates the individual, whereas TV culture short-circuits the development of the concept formation skills needed for higher-level critical and creative thinking by holding the mind in the mode of forming unstable, shallow, and subjective complexes with its confusing and incessant bombardment of the individual with short, disconnected, frenetic messages.

Writing, then, becomes much more important in the new paradigm than a mere skill needed for producing documents in school and at work. It is the key to creative problem solving, innovative critical thinking, and advanced cognitive development. Writing facilitates the generation of new ideas and, in the context of critical cognitive activity, can facilitate the breaking of culturally imposed mental blocks, which limit and restrict thinking.

Writing must be viewed as a problem-solving activity. A writing task should be approached with a strategy for analyzing it and a model for defining stages of the writing process. But precisely what and how material is taught cannot and should not be specified in advance. If teachers understand and are working with the new paradigm, they must create their own courses based not on standardized syllabi or textbooks, but on their own interests and knowledge, materials available, current issues, their students' capabilities and interests, and the constraints of their teaching situations.

Institutionalization of critical cognitive activity begins with the teacher, reversing the current anti-intellectual trend to reduce teachers to mere implementers of policy. Teachers should regain their traditional role as transformative intellectuals "whose function is to conceptualize, design, and implement learning experience suited to the specificity of a particular classroom experience" (Aronowitz and Giroux 1985, 149). Students should be taught to discover power within the education system and the social system. They should be taught to critique and become involved in the popular ideological issues that are now exploited mostly by the conservatives. They should be taught the power of knowledge and the knowledge of power. The new paradigm can be the basis for an agenda that satisfies Aronowitz and Giroux's demand that educators fill the social role of "mediators between the state and everyday life" (1985, 135), giving students an active voice in their learning experience so they can develop "a critical vernacular that is attentive to problems experienced at the level of everyday life" (37).

As Vygotsky suggests, the writing tasks students are given should be connected to real-world problem solving; therefore, if writing is to promote cognitive development and concept formation, writing tasks should function as what Vygotsky calls "leading activities," incorporated into the process of defining and analyzing problems the students have and designing strategies for solving them.

As Aronowitz and Giroux (1985; 1993), McLuhan (1962; 1964), Postman (1985), and others suggest, media studies are a vital part of critical cognitive activity; therefore, as leading activities, students can be engaged in written and spoken analysis of such popular media events as familiar TV shows and commercials, movies, and music, and then move into experiencing the less popular but more innovative media events in film, video, music, dance, literature, and so on, and they can produce their own media events. High culture should be incorporated with popular culture in order to show its relevance to life in today's world.

Students can also be led into the difficult and unfamiliar study of how media have shaped their beliefs, desires, thought patterns, worldviews, and perhaps even brain activities. And, as a needed supplement to expository writing in an age when the image is replacing print, some effort to make important and difficult statements through a montage of mixed media materials or avant-garde art can stimulate creative thinking and make deeper, lasting impressions that may reach an individual's "inner speech" and, eventually, her or his written verbal thought. Much innovative contemporary art incorporates and critiques TV culture. Even the emancipatory potential of TV can be explored through postmodern art theory, video art, and alternative programming.

It is important that all writing activities be connected to larger tasks that are designed to help students learn about the nature of thought and language and society, learn the importance of cognitive skills and mastery of language, learn about the traditional paradigms of gender, sex, race, class, culture, and world underlying our TV culture, and learn to use the new paradigm in developing a language of possibility leading to action.

Though most students need to become more literate, precise, systematic, and logical, they must also be taught to always question the authority of language and to develop a creative and heterogeneous multimedia discourse. For in a world that needs new ways of thinking, invention, not truth, is the goal. This does not mean students should not be concerned about truth, but rather that education should stress the development of the creative, critical, analytical, deconstructive thinking processes needed for coping with the changing world and novel experiences instead of perpetuating a set of absolute truths. Therefore, students must be stimulated to think, not just be instructed, but encouraged to become excited about exercising their creative analytical abilities.

Ironically, two of the most difficult obstacles in teaching critical cognitive activity are the students' inability to think abstractly and analytically in order to *formulate a concept* and to think through a problem creatively, and their inability to *deconstruct a concept* in order to see its limitations and constitutive nature as well as the potential for destablizing, rejecting, or replacing it. As Louis Mackey says, students must be logocentric before they can become deconstructionists. Therefore, two of the main foci in courses that are teaching critical cognitive activity should be the formulation and deconstruction of concepts. Students should learn how they have formed the ideas they have, how to form new ideas, and how to think deconstructively to keep their thinking open and flexible. Since students are likely to be underdeveloped in abstract thinking skills, and since, as Vygotsky says, concepts mature in the mind over time, a considerable amount of time must be spent in these areas throughout the course of their education.

The concluding appendix offers a few of the texts I have used in my courses and how I used them to teach critical cognitive activity. Obviously, there is no end to examples that can be cited as suitable texts for teaching critical cognitive activity. Vygotsky's theory and deconstruction can be made concrete by bringing them into relation to the chosen texts. This is the place of writing. Writing can be resistance against the impotence of our TV culture. Writing is part of the process of finding, developing, and articulating inner speech, that reservoir of internalized thought and language on which we depend for communication. Writing is part of the process of formulating and deconstructing concepts in defining and solving problems. Writing is part of the process of understanding "writing" in the largest sense of producing signification and developing a multimedia language of possibility for confronting the postmodern world.

Even if we assume the worst-case scenario of Orwell and Baudrillard—the disappearance of meaning, the individual, the social, and all the distinctions inherent in the production of signification due to the implosive force of the omnipresent technoloculture that crushes the structure of polar opposites underlying our society—the new paradigm can guide us in repositioning and reconstructing our concepts to reflect our current reality more accurately and to recreate it. Vygotsky's theory and deconstruction show us that these binary opposites are constructions in the first place and, as such, are always already tending to be imploded, since it is only a willful act of intellection that made the distinction in the first place, through the movement of "differance" or the production of signification. After all, the destruction of the old structures of society and reality can be an opportunity to build something new and better based on the new paradigm. Thus, one can deconstruct oneself awake from the nightmares of Orwell and Baudrillard with the Vygotskian process of developing the higher cognitive functions necessary to rethink and recreate the world.

If we are the way Baudrillard says we are, it is only because those of us who were fortunate enough to develop more or less fully as individuals and social beings have allowed ourselves to be programmed and controlled by society rather than performing the difficult mental work necessary to de- or reprogram and control ourselves. But without the assistance of a new form of education structured according to the critical cognitive activity paradigm, it is most unlikely that individuals today can emerge with the concepts and strategies necessary for climbing out of the Baudrillardian abyss.

If individuals are to escape the prison house of image (to borrow Frederick Jameson's metaphor) that is TV culture, education must help them transform themselves into critical cognitive activists. We can try to get there first to lead the way. Let's hurry.

As I finish this manuscript I worry about one of the most appalling epidemics in U.S. history which plagues us today: teenagers amusing themselves to death, literally, with guns. A child dies of gunshot wounds every three hours (Sklar 1993)—in gang shootings, drive-by shootings, shootings for Nikes and Walkmen, and on and on. The test of this new paradigm is to end such self-obliteration. Society has completely failed these teenage gunslingers. What is the effect of seeing 18,000 simulated murders on TV during childhood? What is the effect of growing up in a society with over 200,000,000 guns, making it the most heavily armed and violent country in the world? "It's-only-a-movie-they-know-the-difference-we-can't-have-censorship-well-not-of-violence-maybe-queer-art-oh-and-no-gun-control-sorry-guns-don't-kill-people-you-know-it-says-so-in-the-Constitution-every-body - knows - right - from - wrong - and - I'm - looking - out - for - number-1." What kind of internalized social relations and inner speech does a fourteen-year-old gunslinger have? What stage of cognitive development has he or she reached? Where did he or she first get the idea of killing a person without hesitation or remorse? If we have all been turned into merchandise, images to be consumed, maybe it's easy. In September 1993 President Clinton said we must stop the violence. He said the cost of the status quo was higher than the cost of change. Maybe it's just empty rhetoric. Or maybe he and others in power finally see the new paradigm emerging and realize that we adapt or die. We seem to be in a stage of cultural evolution, on the edge of chaos where things happen, but evolution, contrary to popular myth, is not always improvement. We may not be able to get the beast out of the living room, but we can rechannel its wild destructiveness if a significant part of our society wakes up and fulfills McLuhan's improbable vision of consciously emancipating ourselves from "the subliminal operation of our own technologies" (McLuhan 1962, 95).

> "We, we fragile human species at the end of the second millenium A.D., we must become our own authorization."
> —Julian Jaynes, *The Origin of Consciousness in the Breakdown of the Bicameral Mind*

Appendix: Teaching Materials and Themes for Critical Cognitive Activity

SAMPLE TEXTS

Conceptual Blockbusting: A Guide to Better Ideas
James Adams

This is a text that can be used in many different ways in teaching critical cognitive activity in a variety of different courses. This book presents the whole issue, foreign to most students, of types of thinking, their connection to culture, and the common mental blocks that hinder cognitive development. It is important to focus on blocks early in the course because students tend to have many, not the least of which are writing blocks. Adams, a Stanford engineering professor, writes with the uninitiated student in mind, making the book interesting by using many illustrations and dozens of exercises, many involving writing, to be done in or out of class, all designed to broaden the range of thinking skills. The book also introduces and stresses the concept of "concept" and the importance in problem solving of generating concepts, which could set up a course theme of constructing and deconstructing concepts.

Adams's book can be used to develop mature concept formation and supplemented with texts and discussion about the concepts that are the basis of our culture—how they originated and evolve, whose interests they serve, their value and limitations—and new concepts based on the new paradigm. The whole book serves to explain many of the problems students have with thinking, writing, and problem solving in general. Many of the book's ideas can be applied to the formulation of effective strategies for writing as well as strategies for critiquing the texts of the course.

Dance Hall of the Dead
Tony Hillerman

This is a novel illustrating many of the concepts about thinking and culture in *Conceptual Blockbusting*. Many stereotypes are presented and undermined in this multicultural story, not the least of which are Indian, hero, academic, and police stereotypes. The book works on several planes at once: students are introduced to the complexity of Native American culture and thinking in a realistic and sympathetic way, they read a police story murder mystery of literary depth beyond any they have seen on TV, and they are led to negative criticism of the characters that represent the worst features of the dominant white culture. The conflict of mythologies in *Dance Hall of the Dead* can be analyzed through Barthes's "Mythology Today," in which he reveals the symbolic power of an everyday myth to hold individuals in society in line by unconsciously inculcating them with ideology masking as the natural, innocent, eternal, and true. With *Conceptual Blockbusting* as a resource, students can be given writing and other assignments that require them to analyze characters and events in the novel that exemplify aspects of contemporary American culture.

The Lives of a Cell
Lewis Thomas

This collection of essays exposes many problems and internal contradictions in modern society. Thomas is a model scientist who defies old-paradigm stereotyping in twenty poetically connected essays that touch on many different subjects in an unorthodox style that shifts back and forth from scientific to literary to philosophical as he reconceptualizes science, technology, life, and humanity. He is a model supradisciplinary thinker, a true critical cognitive activist, who creatively critiques society and suggests an alternative to the thinking that produces the fragmented destructive arrogance he sees in today's world; he models the new paradigm presented in chapter 3 with an attitude of humility about the place of humanity, science, and technology in the global scheme and advocates restraint in such areas as nuclear power, based on insufficient understanding of an inherently unfathomable universe.

Nineteen Eighty-Four
George Orwell

To show the need for critical cognitive activity, this famous novel can be used to capture certain features of American culture and the retrograde dialectics of individual and society, thought and language. It is a mistake to teach this novel without adequate preparation, because most students have been victimized in thought and language in just the way portrayed in the novel and, therefore, cannot easily see what is meant and apply it to themselves and their own society. The film *1984* could be viewed, as well as the film *Brazil*, a contemporary update of *Nineteen Eighty-Four* and other popular films that portray dystopic visions, such as *Rollerball, Bladerunner, Videodrome,* and *They Live,* which has a doublespeak theme. Students today are more primed for film than literature, and this may make the message more accessible; moreover, they need to see the superiority of films like these to the *Rambo* and *Star Wars* movies they tend to watch, movies that only reinforce the old paradigm of the simple binary system based on good versus evil and might equals right.

With adequate preparation, *Nineteen Eighty-Four* is a good springboard for advanced and subtle discussion of language, ideology, and culture. The book illustrates Barthes's point that a culture's ideological myths can create a "dead" world that prohibits people from inventing themselves because they refuse language. Myths such as those in the novel, which are distorted reflections of the myths in our society, show the world to be unalterable: there is but one reality, no other, and our myths have captured for all time the essence of truth. There is no politics, no material history, no complexity in the world. Students can be asked to find examples in political rhetoric, advertising, and other reductionist media texts. They can learn a broader definition of politics and learn the political dimension of seemingly neutral activities such as traditional customs, beliefs, language, TV, and technology.

Derrida's critique of logocentrism can be effectively applied to the function of language in *Nineteen Eighty-Four*. Without the critical tools of deconstruction, the function and force of language in the novel are difficult to understand—how a word can mean its opposite, how people can uncritically accept contradictions and force-fed concepts and beliefs, how vocabulary determines thought. Indeed, I am often shocked when an educated person says that Orwell did not get it right, that our problems are not those of *Nineteen Eighty-Four*. If students are to begin to understand the cultural forces that affect them, the nature of language and its role in ideology must be understood. They can be led to identify and deconstruct the conceptual binaries that structure our ideology, such as truth and falsity, good and evil, us and them, individual and society, freedom and slavery. They can see the importance of both mastering and deconstructing language; they can see how unconscious inner speech is formed and how it differs from conscious concept formation and written language. They can be led to see how they themselves have been shaped by the controlling technologies and ideology of society according to the mechanisms explained by Vygotsky's theory and enhanced by current scientific, social, and linguistic research.

Sula
Toni Morrison

This short novel is full of depth, complexity, and texture showing the harsh reality of black American women, and really, women in general, in a way that mass media entertainment never does, even when it says it is doing so. *Sula* is a good text to use in contrast with the misleading if not dishonest images and messages about black women and women in general conveyed in popular culture, for example, on "The Cosby Show" or

"The Jeffersons" or in the film *The Color Purple*. Of course, there are many, many short novels and short stories and poetry by women of all ethnicities from all over the world that can be used to open up many subjects for study, critique, and problem solving.

Frankenstein
Mary Wollstonecraft Shelley

How many people know where the Frankenstein story came from? This incredible novel written by the nineteen-year-old daughter of feminist Mary Wollstonecraft generates enough topics of study and discussion to fill an entire course. A class of mine once filled a large blackboard with themes in an hour. Why don't we know who Shelley is? Why is her husband known and not she? Why are all the many Frankenstein films so bad compared to the book? Why don't many people read the book?

When God Was a Woman
Merlin Stone

This scholarly work and others on the same subject, such as Riane Eisler's *The Chalice and the Blade*, challenge patriarchal interpretations of ancient history by reinterpreting and bringing to light neglected and concealed archeological and anthropological evidence to show that there were many powerful and long-lived goddess cultures in the ancient world that were different in nature from the violent, hierarchical, male-dominated ones we know so well. They may have lived by a different paradigm, the same paradigm behind Eisler's theory which argues, not matriarchy over patriarchy, but "partnership" over patriarchy. Negative reviews of these books can be analyzed deconstructively to reveal ideological and metaphysical biases.

Reflections on Gender and Science
Evelyn Fox Keller

This book shows us that science is not completely objective truth, but the truth that suits ruling-class men. Keller is deconstructing science.

Rocking Around the Clock: Music Television, Postmodernism,
and Consumer Culture
E. Ann Kaplan

This is a very adaptable text with a highly accessible theme. What could engage most young students more than MTV? They are shocked and excited to see it brought into the classroom and surprised to see it taken seriously in an academic setting. Most students have never thought about analyzing MTV, or TV in general. Studying it is a good way to make some points about the need to analyze and critique popular culture. Kaplan's book can be used to introduce students to the concept of postmodernism and to a feminist critique of popular culture.

Kaplan suggests that it may be in respect to MTV that Baudrillard's analysis of culture is most verifiable. The various ideas and attitudes expressed by MTV videos, including politically leftist ones, may be "mere simulacra with nothing *behind*, mere representations, images," because the ideas or values in a particular video become irrelevant as the video becomes nothing but a commodity, a simulation of the "real" beyond the control of producers and performers. All videos become flattened out onto "one continuous present of the twenty-four hour flow," losing all their historical origins. Moreover, most innovative and important music is banned from the venue lest the illusion be broken that there is no such thing as a search for an ideological political position (51–54).

Specifically, Kaplan is concerned from a feminist perspective about the negative effects of MTV, which operates within the patriarchal symbolic. "The reduction of the female body to merely an image is something that women have lived with for a long time. . . . The new postmodern universe, with its celebration of the look, the surfaces, textures, the self-as-commodity, threatens to reduce everything to the image/representation simulacrum." In general she worries about the impact of TV on any potentially subversive or countercultural discourse because of the power of TV to immediately consume it, thereby robbing it of its own identity and power to produce any changes in the dominant culture. "The loss of any position from which to speak—of mechanisms for critical evaluation of social structures and ideologies—that characterizes postmodernism is something to worry about. . . . While there may be a genuinely oppositional youth culture in some European nations, this is no longer true of America. What we have predominately is a uni-dimensional, commercialized and massified youth culture, not really organized by youth itself but by commercial agents, that has absorbed into itself, and trivialized, all the potentially subversive positions of earlier rock movements" (151–152).

Music videos can be shown in class and discussed from Kaplan's and others' points of view. Music genres can be analyzed for their origins, influences, motives, and messages. Genres include rap, punk, hard-core, heavy metal, rock, jazz, country of various types, 1950s, fusion, and so forth. In such activities students are right in the middle of enough issues to keep them busy for a long time, researching, thinking, writing, sharing, comparing, and debating—about something that matters to them.

"Beautiful Red Dress"
Laurie Anderson

This and dozens of other recordings of Anderson are deconstructive, postmodern critiques in sound and poetry (and visuals, on the videos of her performances) of American culture. The cryptic humor, philosophical depth, and artistic originality are a challenge to those who love "cool" music but have never heard anything like this. This particular song is a wry feminist piece about the sexiness of women during menstruation (not a popular subject in music) and the absurdity of depriving women of political power because they menstruate. Anderson is on the cutting edge of popular music coming from the avant-garde scene, which most students know nothing about.

"We Don't Need Another Hero"
Barbara Kruger

This and dozens of other ironic photo/text works in which the text deconstructs the photograph are good examples of the postmodern sensibility, and can lead to discussion of the various ideas that are called "postmodernism."

"Satan, Satan, Satan"
The Butthole Surfers

This and lots of other recordings by the B-Surfers (which they
sometimes have to be billed as because of censorship policies!)
are tear-the-bone-out raging, shocking, disrespectful, anarchistic
hard-core punk rock. They redefine music and art as rebellion,
as Lyotard, for one, says artists always do. This music can lead
a discussion of the punk movement (the postmodern version of
the peace and love hippie movement?) in many different directions. One is the recent famous censorship of Robert Mapple-
thorpe in the United States, the ideological disputes that ensued,
and who was on what side and why. Another is the increasingly
rapid appropriation of the shocking by mass media pop culture,
for example, Madonna. A third direction is the meaning of rejecting the establishment fashion, and a fourth is the meaning of
slam-dancing.

"Burn, Hollywood, Burn"
Public Enemy

This and other rap songs by Public Enemy and others need to
be analyzed in a deconstructive way to get beyond the literalist
self-righteous criticism from some feminists, racists, and law-
and-order folks. This particular song is a witty, insightful, cynical critique of Hollywood, which doesn't, with few exceptions,
include blacks in the power structure or their perspective in
films. "Fight the Power," "Fuck the Police," and "Don't Believe
the Hype," are other angry statements made in the "wrap" of
rap, which occupies a center position in pop culture and global
culture and marks the first time the thoughts and feelings of
American blacks on the streets have been heard and felt so
strongly around the world. Though rap is primarily a male
genre, Ninah Cherry and Queen Latifah are two powerful female
rappers with a feminist message. How can we analyze these cultural phenomena? Do they make a difference? Why do people
fear their influence?

MASS MEDIA SPECTACLES

Certainly no sourcebook is needed on this subject, though there are many interesting and important critiques, the primary one probably being Guy Debord's *Society of the Spectacle*. We are always under the influence of at least one mass media spectacle. On an ordinary day (if, indeed, there are any!), when U.S. presidents aren't being excessively inaugurated for the whole world, or U.S. war heroes aren't being crammed down our throats, or altruistic stars aren't being investigated for child abuse or having a save-the-world extravaganza, or the Statue of Liberty or Elizabeth Taylor isn't having a big birthday party, there's always the latest blockbuster movie being promoted in every conceivable consumer venue known to capitalism. It was *Star Wars*, then *Rambo, E. T., Top Gun, Batman, Dick Tracy, Friday the Thirteenth, Teenage Mutant Ninja Turtles, Dracula,* and *Jurassic Park,* just to name a few of the biggest ones. Promotion appears on posters, lunch pails, T-shirts, video games, video cassettes, key chains, sheets and pillowcases, wallpaper, coffee mugs, baby bottles, hats, bookbags, beach towels, potato chip packages, earrings, dolls, costumes, notebooks, CDs, talk shows, MTV, and more! Debord calls them "pseudo-events," though he wrote that before the mass media spectacle had achieved today's heights. He got the picture early on, as society's visionaries always do. A Situationist International poster reads:

IF WE DO NOT WANT
TO PARTICIPATE
IN THE SPECTACLE OF
THE END OF THE WORLD
WE WILL HAVE TO WORK
TOWARD THE END OF
THE WORLD OF SPECTACLE

This slogan is one way to express the purpose of my book and my project as an educator.

MASS MEDIA IMAGERY: WOMEN, RACE, YOUTH, THE WORLD, THE GOOD LIFE

Of course, this topic intersects with many others, but it can and should be approached as a subject in its own right. It doesn't take long to see what's going on with a continuous blizzard of white, blonde, blue-eyed, young, thin (but healthy, not starving, though in fact the models are often anorexic and sometimes die, but they aren't photographed, one presumes, in the final stages), happy, loved, and prosperous people-images—did I leave anything out? If you don't look very closely, you might draw the conclusion that there are only about ten models in the entire world, because they all look alike. What effect does this have on one's self-image? On the development of one's ideas of beauty and success? On the building of an inner "speech" of imagery? How does this inner imagery connect to the inner speech of thought and language? Where is the heterogeneity of humanity? It is conspicuously and suspiciously absent. But *why?* In whose interests are we told and brutally reminded every waking moment, and doubtless in dream moments as well, that there is only one standard of physical beauty and it is all-important? The CNN we-are-the-world ads, even, are careful not to stray too far from this ideology. Students need to learn to deconstructively analyze all these issues and more. It is interesting how many students resist drawing any negative conclusions about the images in advertising, TV programs, and films. This may suggest that they are already hooked on the ideology/mythology, that the messages have already firmly rooted in their inner thought/ speech/imagery. It took me a entire semester once to convince a group of stubborn sophomores that the film *Teenage Mutant Ninja Turtles* wasn't ideologically innocent just because the heroes look like a cross between a grinning plastic bathtub turtle and Rambo—they're definitely more Rambo than bath turtle. And why is there only one female in the cast of thousands, one who starts out a kind of feminist and devolves into a victimized woman who starts wearing sexy clothes to ensure her salvation by good "men" (?) who solve problems with violence and lovable humor? Funny, though—April (that's the woman's name) started out as pals to the turtles. That should have been enough incentive to help her, but their relationship becomes different the more helpless she gets!

We should connect all this to the increase in violence toward women. Susan Faludi's *Backlash: The Undeclared War Against American Women* and Naomi Wolf's *The Beauty Myth* show the campaign against American feminism at all levels of culture. And we thought only the head-scarved women of Islam had problems, but global culture doesn't give us many images of them.

And aging women have lots of image problems, too. According to Betty Friedan in *The Fountain of Age*, all people who are open to change and who are active with projects evolve. She dispells the myth that aging is a bad thing signifying nothing but decline and deterioration. She shows that, in fact, a very small percentage of old people suffer serious disabilities, that society needs to redefine aging by identifying and measuring the strengths and possibilities of old age: wisdom, potential for deeper intimacies and more fulfilling sex life, potential for developing new broadening facets of oneself. Aging shouldn't be defined as a loss of youth. It is necessary to accept what you are so you can continue growing. Again, this new thinking is a paradigm change that falls under the paradigm change I have outlined—deconstructing the old and creating the new from the insights.

Film

The study of film is an essential aspect of teaching critical cognitive activity. Watching a film is a good leading activity, because students know how to and like to watch films, but they don't know how to "read" them. When people are in a movie theater, they are pretty much a captive audience under the spell of the enormous images and bone-rattling sound. Talk about excremental culture! Hollywood spews its anti-art with the regularity of Old Faithful all over the world. On the other hand, there are brilliant films from Hollywood and elsewhere, old and new—and what a contrast! There are many insightful, deconstructive analyses of films, general and particular, in film journals, books, and even mass media; for example, Douglas Kellner and Michael Ryan's *Camera Politica* and Robin Wood's

Hollywood from Vietnam to Reagan. Classes can go to see a film—
almost any one will do for analytical purposes—and then deconstruct the text. This is an excellent theme for an entire course,
and one that can be easily incorporated into a variety of existing
courses by selecting films that match the course material in some
way. Wood talks at length about feminism—or the lack thereof—
in Hollywood, using two films that are well known and easy to
find on video for close reading, *Alice Doesn't Live Here Anymore*
and *An Unmarried Woman.* These and other essays and films can
be studied and used to lead to other texts and activities.

Popular junk needs to be examined and exposed: the perverse
obsession with violence and the reductionist world of Good and
Evil in which superhuman macho men (sometimes they are
women, which I suppose is progress in the same way that allowing women in combat is) solve all problems with violence, pref-
erably with maximum cruelty, death, gore, fire, explosion,
collision, and destruction—and sometimes macabre humor!
Some of the junk has its (subversive) moments (*Pretty Woman*—
Cinderella's not supposed to be a hooker before she finds her
handsome prince) and aspects (*Basic Instinct*—a woman is not
supposed to be a gorgeous bisexual without morals or conscience
and outsmart all the men). Thankfully, there is an impressive list
of aesthetically and politically brilliant films, some of them even
popular, such as *Thelma and Louise.* Consider *And the Band Played
On*—an act of social responsibility by Home Box Office. Students
can ferret out rare subversive moments on TV like this one,
which is a star-studded docu-drama of the shameful history of
HIV in the United States, a study in homophobia and white male
establishment greed which, it is predicted, will result in around
40,000,000 infected persons by the year 2000.

CNN

"Real Life—Real Drama" "Saving Somalia—Every Night on
CNN"

It is very important to analyze what is happening on CNN in
the light of postmodern theories such as Baudrillard's and
McLuhan's and theories of imagery. What does it mean and
what is the effect of a TV channel advertising itself with images

of starving children every fifteen minutes? And in what sense is this "real life" or "real drama"? CNN claims to be the window on the world for the whole world calling itself the "global news channel"—"We have captured history—live." Students must learn to ask such questions as: Whose worldview is behind these images and messages? *Who is CNN?* How do all the different worldviews around the world understand what they see on CNN? Did they *serve* the world or *capture* it during the Gulf War? And in whose interests? Much of the self-advertising on International CNN is self-congratulatory claims of bringing everyone in the world together in friendship and harmony, with maudlin commercials showing nice faces from "all over the world." Some commercials cheerfully show, with a dizzying blitz of images set to music, all the wars and disasters we have seen so far on CNN. There is much to be deconstructed here.

Propaganda

Students need to learn techniques of propaganda, look for them in advertising, political discourse, and so forth. Take Rush Limbaugh: how does such a person get to be a superstar and be legitimized by the media? Journals like *Propaganda Review* contain useful articles, such as one on Limbaugh, which analyzes excerpts of Bush speeches showing which propaganda techniques he used, something the mainstream media rarely, if ever, does—the analysis revealed twenty-nine propaganda devices in a sixty-five-word excerpt of the State of the Union Address of January 29, 1991. Another article showed how a news text is a constructed narrative with a point of view, showing five versions of one story on five different TV channels in three different countries (all these appeared in issue no. 10, 1993).

Advertising

Teachers and students can find thousands of good examples of TV and print ads that can be analyzed to show the techniques being used for manipulation of various audiences. The images, the people in the ads and what they are doing, must be deconstructed to show what values and emotions are being targeted and whose values and emotions and images are excluded. There are many good articles and artwork that deconstruct advertising, such as Barbara Kruger's photo texts and Lydia Seargeant's monthly column in *Z Magazine*. My mass media imagery entry applies here more than anywhere else.

Montages of Articles from Current Magazines and Newspapers

A good way to show fragmentation and reductionism in mass media is to make a montage or take a found montage from a magazine or newspaper. The sometimes jarring effects of juxtaposion of texts can be analyzed. How do we digest these disconnected bites?

Global Culture

See many of the above items and put them in a global context next to CNN. Film, TV, advertising, music, politics form Images from America—much more powerful than the Voice of America. Global culture is America's number one export, consumer product and political/ideological propaganda all in one. It can be called excremental culture, TV culture, consumer culture, anticulture, simulacrum of culture, friendly fascism. Global culture is a key topic for critical cognitive activity, for people all over the world. The United States is the belly of the beast; therefore, those of us who have seen and survived have a responsibility to discuss and deconstruct it for everyone. Far from being the mythic global village, it is more accurately characterized as the global mall. This is a book-sized topic, and there are many resources of all kinds available, such as Alan Durning's *How Much is Enough? Consumer Society and the Future*; films that critique global culture, such as *The Gods Must Be Crazy*, which brilliantly uses the CocaCola bottle dropping from an airplane into an aboriginal village to symbolize the intrusion of global culture; and the ever-deepening reservoir of the product itself is, of course, omnipresent, if not omnipotent.

After reading this book, I think you can see how a teacher of critical cognitive activity, sensitized by theories and perspectives such as the ones I have presented, plus many more that are and will be available, can use these sample texts and countless others to design an infinite variety of creative leading activities for students at various levels of development in courses with various subject matter. Once you are in the critical cognitive groove, you see hundreds of texts of all kinds every day, old and new, in all media, which, separately or in meaningful juxtaposition, stimulate your imagination for creating interesting and varied classroom activities and assignments. Nothing is too esoteric or too mundane, from the Mandelbrot Set to a T-shirt that screams, NOTHING IS MORE AMERICAN THAN LEVIS!

Bibliography

Adams, James. 1979. *Conceptual Blockbusting: A Guide to Better Ideas*. New York: Norton.

Aronowitz, Stanley, and Henry Giroux. 1985. *Education under Siege: The Conservative, Liberal, and Radical Debate over Schooling*. South Hadley, Mass.: Bergin & Garvey.

————. 1993. *Education Still under Siege*. 2d ed. Westport, Conn.: Bergin & Garvey.

Austin *American-Statesman*. 1993. "Guns Make America a Dangerous Place." (Ann Landers syndicated column), September 19.

Bagdikian, Ben H. 1983. *The Media Monopoly*. Boston: Beacon Press.

Barthes, Roland. 1972. *Mythologies*. New York: Hill and Wang.

Baudrillard, Jean. 1973. *In the Shadow of the Silent Majority*. New York: Semiotext(e).

————. 1983a. "The Ecstacy of Communication." In *The Anti-Aesthetic: Essays on Postmodern Culture*, ed. Hal Foster, 126–135. Port Townsend, Wash.: Bay Press.

————. 1983b. *Simulations*. New York: Semiotext(e).

Bohm, David. 1980. *Wholeness and the Implicate Order*. London: Routledge and Kegan Paul.

Cannon, Carl M. 1993. "Honey, I Warped the Kids." *Mother Jones*. July/August.

Chomsky, Noam. 1980. *Rules and Representations*. New York: Columbia University Press.

Cockburn, Alexander. 1991. "Beat the Devil." *The Nation*, March 18, 330–331.

Conway, Flo, and Jim Siegelman. 1984. *Holy Terror: The Fundamentalist War on America's Freedoms in Religion, Politics, and Our Private Lives.* New York: Doubleday.

Debord, Guy. 1983. *The Society of the Spectacle.* Detroit: Black & Red.

Dennett, Daniel. 1978. *Brainstorms: Philosophical Essays on Mind and Psychology.* Montgomery, Vt.: Bradford Books.

Derrida, Jacques. 1973. *"Speech and Phenomena" and Other Essays on Husserl's Theory of Signs.* Evanston, Ill.: Northwestern University Press.

Durning, Alan. 1992. *How Much Is Enough? Consumer Society and the Future.* Washington, D.C.: Worldwatch Institute.

Eisler, Riane. 1988. *The Chalice and the Blade.* San Francisco: Harper & Row.

Faludi, Susan. 1991. *Backlash.* New York: Doubleday.

Feyerabend, Paul. 1975. *Against Method: Outline of an Anarchistic Theory of Knowledge.* London: Verso.

Foss, Paul. 1984. "Despero Ergo Sum." In *Seduced and Abandoned: The Baudrillardian Scene,* ed. Andre Frankovits. Glebb, Australia: Stonemoss.

Friedan, Betty. 1993. *The Fountain of Age.* New York: Simon & Schuster.

Gitlin, Todd. 1989. "Postmodernism: Roots and Politics." *Dissent,* Winter, 100–109.

Gleick, James. 1987. *Chaos: Making a New Science.* New York: Penguin.

Harris, Daniel. 1990. Boston *Phoenix.* June. Literary section.

Harris, Marvin. 1981. *America Now: The Anthropology of a Changing Culture,* New York: Simon & Schuster.

Harth, Erich. 1983. *Windows on the Mind: Reflections on the Physical Basis of Consciousness.* New York: Quill.

Harvey, Irene. 1986. *Derrida and the Economy of Differance.* Bloomington: University of Indiana Press.

Heidegger, Martin. 1977. *"The Question Concerning Technology" and Other Essays.* New York: Harper & Row.

Hillerman, Tony. 1973. *Dance Hall of the Dead.* New York: Avon Books.

Hirsch, E. D., Jr. 1985. "Reading, Writing, and Cultural Literacy." In *Composition and Literature: Bridging the Gap,* ed. Winifred Bryan Horner, 141–148. Chicago: University of Chicago Press.

———. 1987. *Cultural Literacy: What Every American Needs to Know.* Boston: Houghton Mifflin.

Jameson, Frederick. 1972. *The Prison House of Language.* Princeton: Princeton University Press.

Jaynes, Julian. 1976. *The Origin of Consciousness in the Breakdown of the Bicameral Mind.* Boston: Houghton Mifflin.

Kaplan, E. Ann. 1987. *Rocking Around the Clock: Music Television, Postmodernism, and Consumer Culture.* New York: Methuen.

Keller, Evelyn Fox. 1985. *Reflections on Gender and Science.* New Haven: Yale University Press.

Kellner, Douglas. 1989. *From Marxism to Postmodernism and Beyond: Critical Studies of Jean Baudrillard.* Stanford, Calif.: Stanford University Press.

Kinneavy, James. 1971. *A Theory of Discourse.* Englewood Cliffs, N.J.: Prentice Hall.

Kuhn, Thomas S. 1970. *The Structure of Scientific Revolutions.* Chicago: University of Chicago Press.

Landers, Ann. Syndicated column in Austin *American-Statesman.* September 19, 1993.

Lentricchia, Frank. 1983. *Criticism and Social Change.* Chicago: University of Chicago Press.

Lewin, Roger. 1992. *Complexity: Life at the Edge of Chaos.* New York: Macmillan.

McDonald, Kandice. 1993. "The Cutting Edge: The National Media Literacy Project—New Mexico Breaks Ground with Statewide Pilot Program." *The Independent.* August/September.

McLuhan, Marshall. 1962. *The Gutenberg Galaxy.* New York: New American Library.

———. 1964. *Understanding Media: The Extensions of Man.* New York: New American Library.

Mander, Jerry. 1978. *Four Arguments for the Elimination of Television.* New York: Quill.

Morrison, Toni. 1973. *Sula.* New York: Knopf.

Moyers, Bill. 1989. "The Public Mind: Image and Reality in America." *Consuming Images.* PBS video. Alexandria, Va.

Naisbitt, John. 1982. *Megatrends.* New York: Warner Books.

Nisbett, Richard, and Lee Ross. 1980. *Human Inference: Strategies and Shortcomings of Social Judgment.* Englewood Cliffs, N.J.: Prentice Hall.

Norman, Colin. 1981. *The God That Limps: Science and Technology in the Eighties.* New York: Norton.

Ong, Walter. 1982. *Orality and Literacy: The Technologizing of the Word.* New York: Methuen.

Orwell, George. 1949. *Nineteen Eighty-Four.* New York: Harcourt Brace Jovanovich.

Phillips, Jim. 1993. "Experts Point to Family Life, TV to Explain the 'Chaos.'" Austin *American-Statesman*. August 15.

Postman, Neil. 1985. *Amusing Ourselves to Death*. New York: Viking Penguin.

Propaganda Review. 1993. No. 10.

Reis, Al, and Jack Trout. 1981. *Positioning: The Battle for Your Mind*. New York: McGraw-Hill.

Ryan, Michael. 1982. *Marxism and Deconstruction: A Critical Articulation*. Baltimore: Johns Hopkins University Press.

Ryan, Michael, and Douglas Kellner. 1990. *Camera Politica*. Bloomington: Indiana University Press.

Schwartz, Tony. 1981. *Media: The Second God*. New York: Random House.

Shelley, Mary Wollstonecraft. 1990. *Frankenstein*. Philadelphia: Running Press.

Sklar, Holly. 1993. "The Upperclass and Mothers in the Hood." *Z Magazine*. March.

Spivak, Gayatri. 1976. Translator's Preface to *Of Grammatology*, by Jacques Derrida. Baltimore: Johns Hopkins University Press.

Stone, Merlin. 1978. *When God Was a Woman*. New York: Harcourt, Brace, Jovanovich.

Suleiman, Susan Rubin. 1990. *Subversive Intent: Gender, Politics, and the Avant Garde*. Cambridge: Harvard University Press.

Thomas, Lewis. 1974. *The Lives of a Cell*. New York: Bantam Books.

Ulmer, Gregory L. 1984. *Applied Grammatology: Post(e)-Pedagogy from Jacques Derrida to Joseph Beuys*. Baltimore: Johns Hopkins University Press.

———.1983. "The Object of Post-Criticism." In *The Anti-Aesthetic: Essays on Postmodern Culture*, ed. Hal Foster, 83–111. Port Townsend, Wash.: Bay Press.

Vygotsky, L. S. 1962. *Thought and Language*. Cambridge, Mass.: MIT Press.

———.1978. *Mind in Society: The Development of Higher Psychological Processes*. Cambridge, Mass.: Harvard University Press.

"Washington Week in Review." PBS. September 10, 1993.

Winn, Marie. 1985. *The Plug-In Drug: Television, Children, and the Family*. New York: Viking Penguin.

Wood, Robin. 1986. *Hollywood from Vietnam to Reagan*. New York: Columbia University Press.

Yankelovitch, Daniel. 1981. *New Rules: Searching for Fulfillment in a World Turned Upside Down*. New York: Random House.

Zebroski, James Thomas. 1983. *Writing as "Activity": Composition Development from the Perspective of the Vygotskian School.* Unpublished dissertation, Ohio State University.

Zukov, Gary. 1979. *The Dancing Wu Li Masters: An Overview of the New Physics.* New York: William Morrow.

Index

About the Author

GLORIA GANNAWAY was most recently a Professor at the Institute of North American Studies in Barcelona, Spain. She has also taught at the University of Texas at Austin; Northeastern University; Bilkent University, Ankara, Turkey; Cukorova University, Adana, Turkey; and Austin Community College.